The World's
MOST BEAUTIFUL
Dolls

VOLUME II

First edition/First printing

To purchase additional copies of this book, or to purchase the first volume of *The World's Most Beautiful Dolls*,
please contact:
Portfolio Press, 130 Wineow Street, Cumberland, MD 21502
877-737-1200

Library of Congress Control Number 2001-135272
ISBN 0-942620-53-4

Project Editor: Krystyna Poray Goddu
Design and Production: Tammy S. Blank
Cover design by John Vanden-Heuvel Design
Cover photo: *Madelaine* by John and Angela Barker
Back cover photo: *Lelia* by Hildegard Günzel

Printed and bound in Korea

The World's
MOST BEAUTIFUL
Dolls

VOLUME II

Joan Muyskens Pursley

Portfolio Press

CONTENTS

Introduction

Art dolls—dolls designed and created as art objects for adults—have their roots in the early part of the twentieth century, but didn't really come into bud until the early 1980s. They blossomed in the 1990s, and now are thriving, filling this new twenty-first century with beauty. The early, trailblazing doll artists would be enraptured by the sophistication and artistry of the designs available today. They would also, no doubt, be pleased to discover that dolls have finally and irrevocably entered the arena of fine art.

Dollmaking is one of the most challenging art forms, because it demands such diverse talents. Sculpting, painting, costume design, pattern making, sewing, hair styling and, often, mold making and wig making all go into the creation of a doll. For some artists, it is exactly this multi-skill demand that makes dollmaking so challenging and appealing. Jamie Lynn Williamson, for example, notes: "Over the years, I have enjoyed many forms of creative expression—painting, sewing, drawing. Dollmaking has given me the opportunity to utilize all of my artistic talents to create an art form that almost seems alive."

Helen Cunalta Kish agrees. "There is no other form of portraying the human figure that embodies everything I love to do, other than creating dolls. Fabric, painting, sculpting and overall design—even a little engineering. It's all there in an artist's doll," she says.

Some artists begin with talents in one or two aspects of dollmaking, then learn the other necessary skills, often through tedious trial and error. Such was the case for cloth doll artist Maggie Iacono, who entered dollmaking "through the love of sewing. I was brought up to sew my own clothes since I was nine years old," she says. "I belonged to 4H until I was in high school. Through this club, I enjoyed creating clothing and was taught very well by the sewing instructor, who happened to be my mother. Sewing cloth dolls and their clothing was a very natural outlet. I gradually became frustrated by the more flat-faced two-dimensional dolls that I had made, and began seeking something more realistic. Over many years of trial and experimentation, I came up with the technique I use today. I believe I began as a craftsman and slowly evolved into an artist. I think this is opposite from the way that most dolls artists begin. Most enter into it through having some knowledge of drawing, painting or sculpture of some kind. These are things I have had to learn since starting doll-making."

Another cloth doll artist, Antonette Cely, embraced dollmaking after serving as a costume designer and makeup artist for theater, film and television companies. "I think it was a natural progression for me," says Cely. It was a move from New York City, however, that forced her to find a career outside of the theater. "Making dolls was my answer. I used the same skills, but reduced them in size. I was then able to continue doing what I had always done, only this way I didn't need a theater or production company. I became the producer, director and stage manager, as well as artistic director. It's great, and I really enjoy the freedom."

Marilyn Bolden finds the challenge of turning clay into a portrait very rewarding, but she makes dolls

Jamie Lynn Williamson's doll vignette entitled A Special Moment *is a one-of-a-kind piece made up of two Cernit dolls, both dressed in raw silk.*

Cloth-doll artist Maggie Iacono of Pennsylvania has begun to pair painted furniture with her dolls. This 17-inch doll, named Angelique, *also comes with three felt animals.*

"because people get so much pleasure from them. Collectors love them with such passion. You don't get that from most traditional art."

Carole Piper loves the art form, she says, "because there is never a dull moment with dollmaking. Inspiration is everywhere, and more materials come onto the market every day that can be adapted to making dolls. There is so much talent around in the dollmaking world. I am not a feminist, but I often wonder if a woman might have taken the place of Michelangelo had we not been busy washing the dishes and the baby!"

Artists' Inspirations

Not only must doll artists be adept sculptors who understand the anatomy of the human body, its musculature and proportions, but they are constantly challenged to come up with new faces, new expressions and new personalities for their pieces. If you ask a dozen artists what inspires them,

you may well get a dozen different answers. For instance, Angela Barker gets her inspiration from studying the late-Victorian and Edwardian eras, which she finds "the epitome of costume design. Feminine mystique was at its height, and good manners, taste and style the order of the day," she says. Fortunately, her husband and dollmaking partner, John Barker, has an engineering background that helped him create a unique, jointed doll body that shows off their exquisite period costumes. Also, he's an exceptional sculptor, who can create just the right face for the age and period Angela wants to represent.

Before Nancy Latham begins a new doll project, she says, "I study old photographs, the eyes and the expressions of the children. I fall in love with the child before I create the doll. When collectors look at and hold one of my dolls, I want them to feel the same way I do when I look at old photographs of children," she adds.

"Just about anything inspires me," says Eileen De Vito. "When you love your work as much as I do, it just

Nancy Latham based her 24-inch cloth Amy *on an old photo in her private collection. The doll was a 1999 nominee for a Dolls Award of Excellence.*

Marilyn Stivers surrounds herself with delicate fabrics and sumptuous accessories, which provide inspiration for dolls like her eight-inch Isabeau.

absorbs you, and so many little things you see will spark an idea for a doll. For instance, I get ideas from old paintings in museums and from looking at art books. I love angels, and my daughter will often give me pictures of angels, and they inspire me. But I also get ideas from a length of fabric, a piece of jewelry, even a little knickknack in a gift shop."

Marilyn Stivers finds her own studio a wonderful source of inspiration. "Fabrics, laces and trims spill over and out of numerous drawers. Antique dresses hang on the walls and dolls. Funny little vintage hats with their twisted mesh and folded exquisite flowers find space wherever they can. Jewelry tumbles from old boxes, tables and shelves are adorned with piles of loose beads, and glorious fabrics are spread everywhere—whimsical fabrics, intricately beaded fabrics, bolts of lace, antique fabrics, romantic fabrics, delicate and metallic fabrics, and tulle, tulle, tulle. I'm lucky I have a space left to work in," she says, adding, "Some artists might find this a distraction, but to

me it is a space unlike any other and a constant source of creative energy and delight."

The Making of a Doll

Dolls can be made from many media; wood, papier-mâché, porcelain, wax, cloth, resin, vinyl and polymer clay have all been popular with dollmakers over the years. However, almost no papier-mâché dolls are made today, and wood and wax are uncommon, although there are contemporary artists who use them, including several featured in this book. Cloth dollmaking has been brought to incredible heights during the past two decades, and the polymer clays, known by a variety of trade names, are favorites of many artists who create one-of-a-kind pieces.

Porcelain dolls remain in vogue, and vinyl dolls have improved so significantly in recent years that they have become popular collectibles. Some artists combine several media in one doll. For example, Hildegard Günzel

A few steps in the porcelain dollmaking process are seen in this photo from Ardis. At left is one of her original sculptures; in the center is a just-out-of-the-mold porcelain version of it; and at right is the bust after it was fired, painted and wigged. The unfired procelain piece is a bit smaller because the slip shrinks as it dries, then the kiln firing reduces the size by another twenty to thirty percent.

and Susan Krey make wax-over-porcelain pieces, which have a beautiful glow about them, and Australia's Bev Saxby recently began making leather-over-porcelain dolls.

Porcelain dolls, which account for many of the collectible, limited-edition pieces currently available, begin with original sculptures for the head, arms, legs and, in some cases, the body. Plaster molds are then made from these pieces. Liquid porcelain, called slip, is poured into each mold and allowed to set. The plaster absorbs the liquid from the slip, leaving a clay buildup along the inside of the mold. When the desired thickness is attained, the remaining slip is poured out of the mold, and the mold is allowed to drain. Finally, it is opened and the shell of unfired porcelain, a damp clay called greenware, is gently lifted from the mold. Mold seams are removed, eyes may be cut out and the surface is smoothed; then the piece is fired in a kiln. During this first firing, the piece shrinks up to about thirty percent. After firing, it may be cleaned and sanded once again; after that the painting begins. Pieces

are re-fired in the kiln between the applications of paint. The temperatures required for the firings vary, but may be as high as 2,250 degrees Fahrenheit.

An advantage of working in porcelain is that, once a mold or molds are made, one can replicate the pieces many times. It should be remembered, though, that the process is tedious; each piece of porcelain must be cleaned and painted and fired multiple times. Then the pieces must be assembled. If the doll is large, it often has a cloth body with a wire or metal armature. This must be designed and sewn, and the joints inserted in the limbs and neck. Eyes still need to be inserted, unless the dollmaker has painted the eyes, and the wig must made or selected, styled and applied. While some of the porcelain doll artists featured in this book make editions of several hundred pieces, many make only very small editions of their porcelain dolls; some make just one doll and then destroy the mold.

Making vinyl, resin and poured-wax dolls involves similar steps, although the molds are different

"This twenty-three-inch porcelain doll looked good as a boy and a girl. I couldn't decide which I liked better, so I did both," *says Australian artist Val Ellick about her two versions of* Jordan.

and these media do not require kiln firing. Making vinyl molds is costly, as is the equipment required. While porcelain dollmaking can be accomplished in a home workshop, even a corner of a kitchen, the equipment necessary for making vinyl dolls means they must usually be produced in a factory. The advantage of working in vinyl is that once a master mold is made, one can make unending production molds. Thus, it is easier and less expensive in the long run to produce vinyl dolls than it is to create dolls in porce-

lain. Of course, a vinyl doll does not just pop out of a mold ready made; it, too, must be painted, assembled, wigged and gowned.

Resin, which is a form of plastic, uses silicone molds and needs no firing. Resin dolls can be made in a home workshop, but there are also factories that reproduce artists' creations in resin. Poured-wax dolls, as opposed to those made of solid-wax (which are almost unheard of today), are also made in molds that were initially made

"Zelda is a 22-inch bass-wood creation that I carved in 1995," says Hanna Kahl-Hyland, who makes just two to four dolls a year. "She's a one-of-a-kind and has painted eyes and a mohair wig, and hand-carved hat, gloves and shoes."

from an original sculpture of a difference medium. As in porcelain dollmaking, when the wax reaches the desired thickness against the mold, the still-liquid wax in the center of the mold is poured out, leaving the molded pieces hollow inside. Once the wax pieces are removed from the molds, the artist may do additional sculpting and refining.

Wooden dolls are, obviously, carved one-of-a-kinds. So, too, are the dolls made out of the various polymer clays. These clays, which go by various trade names including Sculpey, Super Sculpey, Sculpey III, Cernit, Fimo,

Promat and Granitex, are man-made substances. Artists work with them just as they would with earthenware, sculpting and modeling their figures. Once the sculpture is complete, the piece must be cured; the advantage is that polymer clays can be cured in a household oven, as the temperature needed to harden the piece is only about 275 degrees Fahrenheit. Of course, it's not just the convenience that draws doll artists to the polymer clays. Some of them have a beautiful translucency that is similar to wax, but the resulting sculptures are much stronger than wax. In fact, dolls made out of the polymer clays are usually as durable as the resin pieces.

Each cloth doll artist has his or her own individual way of working. Some cloth dolls are needle sculpted, that is, tiny stitches are used to pull and tuck the fabric in order to create the desired form. Many cloth dolls, though, begin with a sculpture, just like their porcelain, vinyl, wax and clay counterparts. The sculpture may be used as a form from which a fabric face is molded, or it may be a permanent part of the doll, with fabric stretched over it.

The majority of the artists featured in this book have experimented with various media during their careers. A number of them work in more than one medium. For instance, Pauline Bjonness-Jacobsen, Peggy Dey and Ruth Treffeisen all produce their limited-edition dolls in both porcelain and vinyl. Juanita Montoya, and Paul Crees and his partner Peter Coe make some dolls in wax and some in porcelain. Many artists make limited-edition dolls in porcelain, but use one of the polymer clays—or a mixture of the clays—to create one-of-a-kind pieces.

It should be made clear that when a doll is described by medium, the reference is to the medium used for the doll's head. It does not mean the entire doll is made of that material. A porcelain doll, for instance, may well have a cloth body or, as those made by England's Lynne and Michael Roche, a wooden body as well as wooden arms and legs. Most large dolls have armatured cloth bodies. Smaller designs, and unjointed dolls, may be made totally of one medium. The tradition of identifying a doll's medium by its head is a carryover from past centuries, when dolls' heads were sold separately, sometimes to other companies that finished the dolls, and sometimes to individuals, who then constructed bodies and limbs for the heads, as well as clothing for the dolls.

Just as artists tend to have a preferred medium, so do many collectors. No one medium is superior to another; each has its advantages and its charms. And while collectors may prefer specific media, most base their buying decisions on their personal attraction to the doll, not on the materials used in its creation.

The Business of Doll Artistry

The biggest change in the world of collectible dolls is the number of artists who now create one-of-a-kind pieces. Two decades ago, one-of-a-kind dolls were rare. Even in the early 1990s, a relative handful of artists created only

"*Yvette is one of my tall, slender, elegant fashion ladies,*" says New Zealand artist Jan McLean about this 40-inch porcelain doll, limited to an edition of 35 pieces.

one-of-a-kinds. Today, though, most artists create at least some one-of-a-kind dolls, and many create nothing but one-of-a-kinds. There are several reasons for this trend. The first is the acceptance of dolls as fine art.

In the mid 1990s, dolls began appearing with greater frequency in art galleries; in fact, the artists themselves began organizing prestigious public showings of their and their peers' artworks. Artists created special pieces for these shows, often pushing the envelope on what defines a doll. Publications devoted to collectible dolls gave increased prominence to the one-of-a-kind designs and their makers, giving them international exposure and greater legitimacy.

High-profile collectors of one-of-a-kind works brought added attention to the new art form. Chief among them were actress Demi Moore and fitness advocate Richard Simmons. Not only did they bring attention to doll art, thereby expanding the market for it, but they themselves spent tens of thousands of dollars acquiring artist dolls. Their purchasing power enabled top artists to command fine-art prices for their one-of-a-kind designs. The artists Moore and Simmons admired were encouraged by their financial backing to further experimentation. The knowledge that collectors of means were seriously interested in their work gave these artists greater freedom to challenge themselves.

Surprisingly, large manufacturers and the television shopping networks also contributed to the rise of one-of-a-kind dolls and doll artists. When a company, such as The Ashton-Drake Galleries, Seymour Mann, The Franklin Mint, The Danbury Mint, Sigikid, Ganz or Götz, works with doll artists to reproduce their designs in porcelain or vinyl, the artists are freed from worrying about the production and business aspects of dollmaking. That freedom, coupled with the security of an income from the sale of the mass-produced dolls, allows the artists to do what most of them love best: design and sculpt. The same is true when doll artists work with QVC or Home Shopping Network. Rather than compete with these corporations, most artists who design dolls for large companies either produce their own dolls in a different medium, keep their edition sizes very small or issue one-of-a-kinds only.

Being A Smart Collector

As a collector, you should bear in mind that your dolls are art. In addition to handling them with care, you should record your purchases, keep your receipts, and if a piece is costly, consider insuring it, just as you would a piece of good jewelry or a painting. Historically, dolls with their original boxes have brought higher prices at auction than dolls without boxes. This is, in part, because the boxes helped collectors identify antique dolls, and is particularly important for dolls of the modern era (1945-1970). Today, most artists mark their dolls in some way, generally under the wig or on the back of the neck, so having a box isn't always as important. However, like their antique ancestors, contemporary dolls with boxes sell for more and faster than those without. So if you have the storage space, keep those doll boxes on hand. Even if you know you'll never sell your dolls, your heirs might.

A record of previous owners of a piece, called a provenance, also ups the value of anything for sale on the secondary market. For some reason, while today's collectors may be adamant about keeping those cumbersome boxes, few provide their dolls with provenances. This is easy to do and can be fun, too. At the very least, keep a list of the dolls you own and when and where you bought each

Verena is a 26-inch-high porcelain doll by German artist Ruth Treffeisen, who is known for her tender depictions of children. The doll is limited to an edition of 35 pieces.

one, along with the purchase price. (Ideally, you will have the receipt of purchase to keep with your list.) An even better idea, however, is to have someone take photos of you and each of your dolls. Better still: if you have a chance to meet an artist at a store or show, have a photo taken of yourself with the artist and the doll. Date the photos; add a little note about yourself, the doll and when you purchased it, and put the photos and notes with your other records. Of, if you prefer, keep the photos and notes in the dolls' boxes, along with any papers that came with the doll, such as a certificate of authenticity and receipt of purchase. These visual records will provide you and your family with happy memories in years to come, and they just may travel through the centuries with your dolls, to be pored over and enjoyed by future generations of collectors and museum curators.

"*Suu is a Chinese girl, four years old, sitting for a snapshot,*" explains well-known German artist Rotraut Schrott. "*She wears an old Chinese hat, colored silk dress and shoes with dragon faces.*" The 32½-inch doll is a Cernit one-of-a-kind, as are all of Schrott's pieces.

Norwegian artist Sissel Bjorstad Skille describes her 30-inch-high one-of-a-kind Simone *as "a neighbor girl, wearing a knitted cotton jacket in a Norwegian design, and carrying an old doll. Her dress and apron are also cotton. Her head, arms and legs are Modelene, while her body is made of cloth, wool and a plastic skeleton."*

16

The Dolls & Their Makers

Author's Note

In 1995, Karen Bischoff and I compiled and wrote a book titled *The World's Most Beautiful Dolls*. That book, conceived by Robert Campbell Rowe, president of Portfolio Press and publisher of *Dolls* magazine at that time, is now in its third printing. The world of dolls, however, has grown and changed greatly since its publication, and so Krystyna Poray Goddu, editor in chief of Portfolio Press, believed a new volume of the book was due. I was delighted when she asked me to do this second volume, and have had great fun, as well as a gread deal of angst, in putting it together. There are so many wonderful doll artists working today that it was extremely difficult to choose whom to include. I felt it was important to show dolls in a variety of media, to show dolls of both children and adults, and finally, to show affordable, mass-produced examples as well as one-of-a-kinds that few of us will ever be able to purchase. Many of the artists included are featured in the earlier volume, but also well represented are new artists who are creating remarkable works. The following pages highlight the world's most beautiful dolls; fortunately for collectors, these are but a sampling of the infinite creations that could fill this volume. — *Joan Muyskens Pursley*

I made my first doll from a clothespin when I was about five. I made my next one in the late 1980s," says Ardis Shanks, known in the art and doll world by her first name only. "I've been a professional artist for about forty years. My husband and I divorced when our four children were young, and I supported them and myself with my art. I did free-lance work for a foreign news service, taking photos of everything from presidents to satellites on launch pads. I did designs for a Christmas decoration company. And I painted portraits and worked as a sculptor, often reproducing my work in bronze."

Some of her clients suggested she make dolls, to which she'd scoff, "I'm a professional artist, not a toy maker." Then one day a client gave her a few doll magazines. "I discovered that some dolls looked like 'art,' so decided I'd try to make just one. I wasn't happy with the results, so I kept trying, making just one more. Now I have almost no time for portrait work, as I continue to make just one more doll."

Ardis was born in Tahlequah, Oklahoma, but moved around quite a bit during her childhood, as her father's job with the Boy Scouts of America took him from Oklahoma to Pennsylvania, New York and Delaware. She was always interested in art and never thought of being anything other than an artist. "I remember drawing trees when I was in kindergarten, trying to make them look real. I also recall being punished in the first grade when, after a spelling test, our teacher told us to use the remaining space on the paper for what we felt we needed to practice most. I drew a line of the best trees I could. When the teacher saw them, she made me stand in the corner; I guess I was supposed to be writing the correct spelling of words I'd missed," she says, smiling at the memory.

Encouraged by her parents, Ardis took art classes in high school, and then spent a year at Moore College in Philadelphia and a year at the University of Michigan, Ann Arbor. Her most valuable training, though, came from private classes with Italian sculptor Renzetti and painter Frank Schoonover—classes she took at the suggestion of Norman Rockwell. "Rockwell was doing a lot of painting for the Boy Scouts of America when my father was working in the national office in New York City," Ardis says. "When dad showed Mr. Rockwell my artwork, he said I should study painting with either N.C. Wyeth or Frank Schoonover, and drawing from life and sculpture with Renzetti. Dad chose Frank over N.C. because he was nearer to our home." The skills she learned from these artists have served her well throughout her career and are obvious in her stunning dolls.

Ardis has created dolls depicting children, but most of her porcelain pieces feature dreamy young women, almost fantasy figures. Her dolls begin as clay sculptures. "I use a non-drying clay for pieces that are 21 inches and less, and real clay for the occasional larger piece," she says. After the original sculpture, she makes her own molds, then casts the piece in porcelain. She also does all the cleaning, firing and painting of her dolls, designs and makes their costumes, and fashions their wigs. Prices for her pieces begin at $1,500.

Bird Woman, 21 inches, porcelain

I have been making dolls since early childhood," says English artist Angela Barker. Inspired by her mother, a tailor who also made and sold dolls at local fairs, young Angela's first dolls were created from socks and handkerchiefs. At age fourteen, she was given her first sewing machine and "progressed to clothes making." She was also a talented artist, and was privately tutored by Valerie Churm, Art Lecturer at Huddersfield University. She didn't envision a career in the arts, however, so studied shorthand and typing, and did office work until her marriage to John Barker.

Angela returned to cloth dollmaking when the couple's children were young. "I first discovered porcelain dollmaking in 1985 whilst on holiday in South Africa. I knew this was something I had to do," she says. Once back in England, she and John bought a kiln, molds and slip, and taught themselves how to make porcelain dolls. Angela's early porcelains were re-creations of the early French bébés. She first sold her dolls in 1988.

John Barker was also introduced to dolls and crafts at an early age. After World War II, his parents made and sold rag dolls, teddies, rabbits, jewelry and other handmade gift items, which he would help make during school holidays. When he was twelve, he began making hand puppets and later turned to more elaborate string puppets. "He made enough of them to put on shows, but he soon got tired of this, so he made his stage set into a counter and sold all the puppets to neighborhood children," says Angela.

John attended Engineering Bradford College, but his interest in cars led him to join a friend in establishing a classic car restoration business. In 1989, his partner moved to Australia, and rather than continue the business alone, John decided to work with Angela. "When John began to sculpt, I wasn't very supportive, as I loved my early work so much," says Angela, "but as we worked more closely together, we created the look for which we are now known."

When John began creating dolls that were perfect for period costuming, Angela was able to concentrate on her lifelong passion for costume design. Today, John does all the sculpting of their dolls. In addition, he has developed a unique doll body. "The development of our bodies has been continuous," says John, whose background in engineering helped him to make a unique lady body in 1996, and more recently, a twelve-piece body with rolling shoulders and hips. "The stringing was an absolute nightmare, but eventually succumbed to John's obstinate will," adds Angela.

The couple—members of the prestigious British Doll Artists Association—create just five or six new designs each year. They do a few one-of-a-kinds, which sell for $10,000 each, but issue most of their dolls in editions of fifteen to twenty pieces. About 30 to 40 inches high, the dolls have porcelain heads and arms, and tension-strung, articulated composition bodies. They wear late-Victorian or Edwardian era outfits constructed from lush fabrics. Thirty-nine-inch *Madelaine*, shown on the cover of this book, is dressed in an Edwardian evening gown in beige silk, overlaid with black and beige French lace. Its overskirt is cut to drape into soft pleats and folds, and narrows at the ankles. The hem is trimmed with black velvet and opens to reveal the front panel of the foundation skirt, made of pleated silk and tulle.

Belinda, 29 inches, porcelain; Inset: *Carmen*, 39 inches, porcelain

When Swiss artist Maja Bill-Buchwalder thinks of childhood playthings, her first doll and its "sad fate" come instantly to mind. It was a little rag doll that she had made, a cuddly piece she insisted upon taking with her when she was hospitalized for several days, and which the medical staff threw out for "hygienic reasons." Many other dolls— some made by her mother, others purchased—were a part of her youth, but none was as loved as that first doll.

Bill-Buchwalder cannot explain the special love she felt for that doll, nor can she explain what draws her to create dolls today. After completing her education, she taught nursery school and, in 1972, she began making cloth dolls for the children in her classes. Later, she made dolls for her own children. She switched from cloth to leather, she says, "when my children began to smear the faces of their darlings with cream." In an effort to capture the faces of her children on her dolls, the mother of four began to model them in clay. In 1980, when her daughter broke one of these pieces, Bill-Buchwalder bought her a Sasha Morgenthaler doll, and turned her own focus to creating dolls for adults.

If other Swiss were making collector dolls at that time, Bill-Buchwalder didn't know them. In fact, "collector dolls" was not a term she had heard. She was very isolated in her pursuits and made many errors, but didn't stop experimenting. She worked with clay, Cernit, Fimo, Plasticine, papier-mâché and wax. She tried making mechanical dolls, and she bought bag after bag of plaster in her attempts to make molds. Eventually, she learned about other artists who were making dolls for adults. Then she met Hildegard Günzel, whose dolls inspired her to consider porcelain. Another dollmaker, Lothar Grossel, taught her how to make molds. Unfortunately, she had no one to turn to for advice on how to use a kiln, so once again she went through a period of trial and error as she struggled to find the correct temperatures for firing her porcelain pieces. But she hadn't come so far to fail, and once she'd mastered her equipment, she began winning awards for her dolls and having them included in prestigious exhibits.

Today, Bill-Buchwalder has someone else make her molds, and she has assistance in sewing her dolls' costumes, but she does all the rest of the work on her pieces by herself. She sculpts in clay, and then reproduces her dolls in porcelain editions of just ten pieces. Each of these is usually a bit different, because she "works each one while the clay is still damp." Also, she may costume dolls in the edition differently. The artist loves fabrics, old and new, and admits to having a "massive collection" of material which she enjoys digging into for her dolls. The two versions of *Huiping* are typical of her work. Not only has she dressed these 32-inch dolls differently, but there are also subtle differences in the way they've been painted (notice the eyebrows). The dolls' mouths appear slightly different, too.

In addition to making her own dolls, sold under the name Maja Bill, the artist designs dolls for Sigikid, a German toy company, which reproduces them in vinyl. Bill-Buchwalder also creates contemporary sculpture and has written a charming book about her journey into dollmaking. Titled *Facets of Doll Art*, it was published by Verlag Puppen & Spielzeug, Duisburg, Germany.

Huiping (2 versions), 32 inches, porcelain

Pauline Bjonness-Jacobsen

I always enjoyed creating things, even as a little girl," says Pauline Bjonness-Jacobsen, whose ability to find pleasure in creativity helped her through some difficult early years. The daughter of a Dutch ship captain, she was born in Makassar, Indonesia, and was among the 150,000 Dutch people on the island of Java when it was invaded by the Japanese in 1942. All were sent to concentration camps. Her father was sent to one camp, her eleven-year-old brother, to another; the artist, her mother, sister and younger brother were imprisoned in Halmahera. Bjonness-Jacobsen found mental escape from the camp's horrible conditions by making toys shaped from mud and hardened in the sun.

At the end of World War II, the family was reunited. All had survived, although Bjonness-Jacobsen and her mother were malnourished, in addition to having malaria and pneumonia. When they were well enough to travel, the family moved to The Netherlands. Bjonness-Jacobsen spent her teens there and at school in Switzerland. After high school, she hoped to go to Rotterdam's Academy of Art (she'd had painting lessons from one of the Academy's well-known artists, Aat Leflang), but her parents were returning to Asia and wanted her with them. They settled in Hong Kong, where Bjonness-Jacobsen studied Chinese painting.

"I always loved to draw and paint, particularly young children and babies. When I was eleven or twelve years old, I made my first tiny cloth dolls using stocking material for their heads and limbs. I stuffed the bodies and embroidered little faces. I used pipe cleaners as armatures and dressed these little dolls with leftover brocade and laces that I found in my grandmother's sewing chest." During her teens, she concentrated on painting; however, she return to dollmaking shortly before her marriage.

"I visited Norway to meet my fiancee's family, which included my future sister-in-law and her little girls. After I came home, I busily got to work and sewed some cuddly, soft cloth dolls with hand-painted faces and yarn hair." The making of these gifts revived her interest in dolls, and in the early 1970s, when she and her husband, Mick, opened a gift shop in Hong Kong, she began selling some of her cloth dolls in the store.

Always experimenting, Bjonness-Jacobsen moved from making cloth dolls to porcelains and, eventually, vinyls. Because of the demand for her designs, she formed Pauline Collectibles, the company that now issues all of her creations and has become a family business. "My elder son, Mikkel, and I jointly share in the sculpting. My daughter, Liesbet, helps with concepts and development of the accessories, and my younger son, Ernst, handles the day-to-day marketing of the dolls," the artist says.

Bjonness-Jacobsen's main subjects are babies and children. "I am fascinated by the sweetness and innocence of children. They are so full of imagination and wonder, and I love being around them. I feel very peaceful and relaxed with them, and it's probably why they truly are my favorite subject to draw, paint and sculpt." Having experienced so many cultures during her childhood, she is especially adept at portraying children of various ethnic backgrounds; she has created delightful dolls of European, American, Asian, African and Alaskan children. Most are issued in editions of 500 to 3,000 pieces. All are noteworthy for the beauty of their facial features and the quality of their costumes, made primarily from fabrics from the United States and the United Kingdom.

Mikayla, Nicola Huisan, Isabel, each 22 inches, porcelain

After a sixteen-year partnership with artist Susan Snodgrass, in 1996 Stephanie Blythe began working alone, creating delicate fantasy characters that are charming collectors around the world. Since that time, the artist says, "I have been on a journey to find a new expression, while continuing to create dolls that awaken the joy, spirit and imagination of childhood. I am exploring feelings of romance, sensuality, power and passion.

"Learning to make dolls has been an evolutionary process. I am still learning," she says, noting that when she and Snodgrass began making dolls together in 1979, they used porcelain parts made by Sylvia Mobley. "Eventually, Sylvia taught me the traditional porcelain dollmaking process, and over the years I have created my own style and techniques." For example, as her art has evolved, she has abandoned the flesh-colored porcelain slip she used to make her dolls. "I now prefer white porcelain and use washes of flesh-colored china paint to create more depth in the painting. Although I make molds for my work, I individually sculpt each clay piece after it is removed from the mold. In this way, I can give each a unique character, and the movement and expression of the figure is not limited by the restrictions of my mold making," she explains.

"Each costume emerges, often intuitively, from a variety of textures and patterns of decorative elements collected from every place and every decade of the past one hundred years: silks, velvets, laces, crystals, metallic threads, butterfly wings, miniature seashells. Often these elements are changed by cutting, dyeing, painting, folding—whatever works. Although my work is small in scale, I enjoy including intricate detail, so that living with my work is contemplative and a constant discovery."

Blythe was born in Berkeley, California, but spent most of her youth on the Eastern seaboard, in Maryland and New Jersey. In 1963 and 1964 she lived in France and Israel, where her father was a visiting professor; while in Israel, she attended Jerusalem's Bezalel Art Academy. She also attended the Philadelphia College of Art, where she earned a B.F.A. degree, and the University of Santa Monica, where she earned an M.A. in applied psychology. Before making dolls, she spent a year in New York City designing scarves and sheets for the manufacturer Vera, then married and had two children. After twenty-five years on the East Coast, Blythe returned to California, where she now lives with her second husband, Dean Walters.

"My goal is to create a beautiful work of art that will inspire an awakening of dreams, memories, stories and longings through the tactile, the sensual, the unexpected and the surprising," says Blythe, whose mermaids and little, three-inch *Pansies* are shown here. The artist has won a number of awards for her dolls and had them featured in numerous magazines and books. They have also been included in many prestigious exhibits and can be found in the permanent collections of Washington Doll's House & Toy Museum, Washington, D.C.; The Miniature Museum of Kansas City, Kansas City, Missouri; Musée Des Arts Décoratifs, Palais Du Louvre, Paris, France; Rosalie Whyel Museum of Doll Art, Bellvue, Washington; Delaware Toy & Miniature Museum, Wilmington, Delaware; and The Carol & Barry Kaye Museum of Miniatures, Los Angeles, California. Blythe is a member of the National Institute of American Doll Artists, the American Craft Council, the 101 Doll Club and the United Federation of Doll Clubs.

A Tall Tale, 4½ and 9 inches, porcelain

Pansies, 3 and 7 inches, porcelain

27

*M*y older sister, who is now a fine portrait artist, was always drawing or painting when I was a child," says Marilyn Bolden. "I would constantly watch her and try to imitate what she was doing. However, I never seemed to come close to her skill. Still, I kept trying, and eventually I developed my own style. I went from drawing horses to cartooning to a love for fashion design. I drew clothes for 'Katy Keene' as a child, and even had one of my designs published in one of her comic books, which was a great thrill for me."

Bolden studied art in college and took some courses in fashion design, but chose marriage over a career. She and her husband, Alex, had two children, Bret and Dawn. Sadly, Dawn was hit by a car and disabled when she was just two years old. Bolden spent the following years taking care of her and dabbling in various arts and crafts. "In addition to drawing and painting, I attempted batik, stained glass, embroidery and quilting, and made many stuffed animals."

When her daughter died at the age of sixteen, Bolden turned to her art for solace. "I found a doll magazine in a doctor's waiting room and was amazed to see that people actually made dolls. I had not sculpted since college, but I bought some Sculpey and tried to make a doll's head," she says. "Sculpting became an outlet for my grief. I became so engrossed that I forgot everything else." Initially, Bolden created one-of-a-kind portrait dolls, but in 1990 she began making limited-edition porcelain pieces. Today, she creates both one-of-a-kind and limited-edition dolls; their heights range from about 25 to over 40 inches. Her one-of-a-kinds sell for $1,200 to $2,000; dolls issued in editions of between five and one hundred are priced from $250 to about $1,400. Using Super Sculpey, Bolden creates about five original sculptures a year. All of these are used to make molds for porcelain dolls, whether they will be one-of-a-kinds or issued in limited editions.

Although Bolden has a great flair for fashion, and her dolls are beautifully costumed, her favorite part of dollmaking is doing the original sculpture. The worst part of the process, she says, is selling her dolls. "I'm so close to them by the time I'm finished, each doll is made with such love, that it's almost like putting your own child up for sale."

When discussing her artistic style, she says, "My dolls could be described as idealized realistic. I like to think they have soul. While I think my dolls are sweet and pretty or cute, I try to capture a personality in each, rather than strive for beauty." The artist has sculpted "everything from babies to a couple in their eighties." Most of her pieces, however, are of young girls or girls in their early teens, and generally their faces have a hint of a smile. "It's uplifting for me to sculpt a face that is ready to smile," explains Bolden, "and I hope it's uplifting for people who look at them, too."

Bolden's dolls have been nominated for a number of awards and featured in national consumer magazines. Her *Molly at 16* was a 1995 DOTY award winner, and her *Rose* was honored by *Dolls* magazine with a 1998 Award of Excellence.

Yvette, 42 inches, porcelain; Inset: *Eliana*, 32 inches, porcelain

I enjoy the challenge of trying to make a realistic image from cloth," says Antonette Cely. "Once I come up with the idea, the only fun part is making the doll as real as possible. Other than that, it is all hard, boring work. If I could make a doll in one day, I would do it. But on this level of work, it takes weeks, sometimes months."

Cely begins her dolls by dyeing cotton broadcloth to a light skin tone. Next, she sculpts a face from Sculpey III or Fimo and covers it with the cloth. The eyes are cut out of the fabric to reveal the polymer clay; then, they are "painted and varnished to give them a realistic shine." The doll's body and limbs are made from cotton broadcloth stuffed with polyester fiberfill. Cely uses a pipe-cleaner armature in the hands only. "If the doll stands by herself," she says, "there will be a brass armature running up through the leg to the knee.

The brass goes down through the foot into a wooden base and is threaded at the end, secured by the use of a nut. In this way, the doll is bolted to her base." Her dolls range in height from 16 to 18 inches and most have mohair wigs. "Every doll is another attempt to improve the techniques, patterns, etc., to make a doll that looks like a real person," says the artist.

Born in Michigan, Cely spent her early years in that state, and her teens in Arizona. She atttended Vassar College, where she majored in French. After graduation, she moved to New York City and found work in the theater. She became Playwrights Horizons' resident costumer, and also worked as a costume designer and makeup artist in film and television. In 1982, while working on a film that called for an eighteenth-century doll, her research on what it should look like piqued her interest in dolls and their history.

Later, she found a book on Japanese dolls in the Lincoln Center Library for the Performing Arts. "It was just sitting on top of books on stage makeup, which I was researching to prepare for a commercial for which I was going to have to do Cliff Robertson's make-up. I was nervous about it, so went to the library for help. I leafed through the makeup books, but I took the Japanese doll book home and started playing with the patterns in it." Shortly after that, Cely moved out of New York City and began devoting her time to cloth dollmaking. She became a member of the Southern Highland Craft Guild and was also elected to the National Institute of American Doll Artists.

In addition to making truly incredible cloth dolls, Cely has been a columnist for *The Cloth Doll Magazine*, written articles for several other publications, published two books and two doll patterns, and produced doll seminars. What she really wants to do, though, is write and direct "the great American film. My greatest fantasy is to be at Sundance Film Festival someday with my own original film. While I am still learning the craft of writing screenplays, I do have several projects that are in one stage of completion or another. One of them—a horror film—actually includes a dollmaker as the protagonist! She uses her dollmaking skills to fight off evil spirits. To find out more, you'll just have to see the movie. Coming (not very soon) to a theater near you!"

Decisions, Decisions, 16 inches, cloth

Diversions—Music, 16 inches, cloth

Midnight Rendez-vous, 16 inches, cloth

Anna Chapman

"As far back as I can remember, I have created my own dolls," says Anna Chapman, who was born and raised in Grundy, Virginia. "As a child in the mountains of Virginia, I used the materials at hand—including rocks and interestingly shaped stones." Life in rural Virginia was not easy for Chapman, who married at an early age. She and her husband moved to Ohio, and she went to work in a factory. She went from making bullets for the armed services' M-16 rifles to making toys at the Ohio Art Company.

Her first marriage ended in divorce, and as a mother of two, she moved to Florida, where her own mother was living. It was there she met Jim Chapman, to whom she has been happily married for more than thirty years. With his support, she went to Florida State College and earned an R.N. degree. As a licensed practical nurse, Chapman worked at Baptist Medical Center in Jackson for about seven years. With the birth of two more children, she left nursing and became active in state politics and charitable endeavors.

She also once again had time for doing crafts. "As a young mother I made cloth dolls by hand for my small daughters. As my children grew, I was able to devote more time to my artistic pursuits. I found a local shop where I could learn dollmaking, and took classes through Seeley's and Bell's [companies that produce doll molds]. In 1988, I began producing antique reproduction dolls." Chapman enjoyed working with porcelain, and opened her own shop to sell dollmaking supplies and teach reproduction dollmaking to others. Shortly thereafter she decided to invite doll artists to give sculpting seminars in her store. Among them were Jack Johnston and Hildegard Günzel. Chapman joined her customers at their seminars and discovered her own talent for sculpting, a talent these artists encouraged.

Chapman began sculpting her own dolls in 1994, and sold her first piece the following year. Today, she still has her store, but opens it just one day a week, when she gives dollmaking classes to area hobbyists. The rest of her time is spent at her dollmaking or enjoying her family, which now includes six grandchildren. These little ones inspire her work, as do the children of friends and acquaintances. "I have always loved children," the artist says, "and especially enjoy youngsters between the ages of one and seven. They take such joy in discovering the world around them, they're so innocent and so easily pleased at that age. I feel such awe when looking at a child—marveling at the perfection from our Grand Creator. I am overwhelmed with gratitude to have been gifted with the talent required to represent this perfection from a piece of clay," she adds.

Chapman sculpts about six new dolls a year, which she issues as limited-edition porcelains. Her editions are small, ranging from eight to twenty pieces; she also makes some one-of-a-kinds. Chapman loves to work with natural fabrics, which she uses exclusively for her dolls' costumes. *Eden Learns to Dance* is typical of Chapman's delicate porcelain children. The doll is 29 inches high, limited to an edition of twenty, and costumed in a silk dress trimmed with 100-percent cotton lace, and silk slippers.

Eden Learns to Dance, 29 inches, porcelain

*M*ost people, when they come upon something that fascinates them, think "how wonderful" and get on with their lives. A few inspect the object and wonder how it was made. Angela Clark went one step better. When she saw her first collectible doll, a realistic vinyl baby from Germany that had her in awe, she turned to her husband and asked if he could sculpt. A teacher and commercial artist, who specialized in illustration and painting, he said, "Sure." So Angela decided they would become dollmakers.

Actually, Steve Clark had never sculpted, and when he began work on his first doll, he discovered it was not easy. But he comes from a tenacious family and, once started, wasn't about to give up. Eventually, he completed a doll that both Clarks agree was quite terrible; but they enjoyed the challenge—Angela designed and made its clothing—and in 1991, within a year of their first stab at dollmaking, they were selling their creations. Today, the Clarks are among their country's top doll artists, and have an international following.

Born and raised in Australia, the couple resides in a small town about a hour south of Sydney, in the Southern Highlands of New South Wales—"a beautiful, pictur-

esque part of Australia." They have three daughters—Holly, Hannah and Charlotte—who, with their friends, inspire the Clarks' work, as do "faces in magazines, advertising, movies, anywhere," says Steve. "The attraction of a particular subject involves character and personality more than features, because our interest is in realism—and probably heavily influenced by living with three daughters and their moods. We use body language, combined with facial expression, to tell a small story. We hope that all of our dolls encourage people to imagine the circumstances that led to that particular character, such as what caused a pout, a smirk, a sad or reflective expression. Also," says Angela, "my love of classical fiction and art is a heavy influence in our choice of adult characters."

The Clarks' dolls represent two age groups: children between the ages of four and fifteen, and young adults in the twenty- to twenty-five-year age range. They create three or four new dolls a year and issue them as limited-edition porcelains. Editions may be as small as five, for a lady doll in a complex costume, to a maximum of forty. Steve does the sculpting, mold making and painting of their pieces, and Angela assembles the dolls, and does all the clothing design, pattern making and sewing. "I inherited a love of fabric and color from a wonderful great-grandmother, who happily lived to the age of ninety-three and was the Saturday afternoon alternative to watching football with my father and brother. She was an avid quilter, and patient enough to teach me," says Angela, adding, "My mother claims that she is 'artistically challenged'—she is a mathematician and can add faster than any person I have ever met."

The Clarks' artistic goal is to produce "a beautifully crafted piece of art, incorporating excellence in scale, design and finish. Our approach is painstaking and slow, but we hope the results make the effort worthwhile." The Clarks do all the work on the dolls themselves, although they do have a small team of skilled craftspeople who produce eyes, shoes, hats, bags, bears and a variety of accessories. Typical of the couple's work, *Eleanor* and *Thomas* represent siblings.

Eleanor and *Thomas*, 31 and 30 inches, porcelain

Elizabeth, 36 inches, porcelain

Kate and *Annie*, 32 and 31 inches, porcelain

erdine Creedy was in her forties when she discovered contemporary artist dolls, and they changed her life and her family's. Born in the little country town of Moorreesburg, South Africa, and raised on a wheat farm, Creedy had no formal art training. She enjoyed handicrafts as a child, but chose grade-school teaching as a career, attending South Africa's Paarl Teachers' Training College. At the age of twenty-four, she married Mike Creedy, an electro-technical engineer. In 1986, pregnant with her fourth child, she decided to leave teaching and find work she could do from home. She had made pottery for a decade, and was sculpting busts when she discovered molds for making reproductions of antique dolls. She enjoyed making these dolls, but was frustrated that they "didn't look like real children." Then she found molds for contemporary dolls, and began making and selling them.

The turning point in Creedy's career came in 1993, when a friend invited her to go Germany's Nuremberg Toy Fair, where she met Hildegard Günzel, Ruth Treffeisen, Sonja Hartmann and Annette Himstedt. Captivated by the beauty of their dolls, Creedy knew that she wanted to create original artist dolls, too.

It took only one doll sculpture for her to know she'd found her forte. Recognizing her talent, her husband dedicated himself to helping her realize her dream of creating beautiful dolls. Because of the difficulties of exporting porcelain dolls to America, where most of her dolls were being sold, the Creedys thought about moving to the United States. They were able to do so when they "won" the United States' green-card lottery in 1996. "When we came here, we didn't know anybody, so my husband and our children all started working in the 'business,'" the artist says. Her husband makes her molds. Their eldest child, Charlene, cleans and assembles the dolls; their three sons handle a variety of general tasks. Back in South Africa, Creedy's mother, Helene Smit, lends a hand. A watercolor painter by profession, she does the crochet work that adds such charm to the dolls' costumes.

Most of Creedy's dolls depict young girls, about the ages of the children she used to teach. "Little girls this age are so interesting, and they do such funny things. You can bring that into your dolls. Of course, unlike the children I used to teach, the children I create are very good. They don't talk back," says the artist. She generally knows exactly what she wants a doll to look like before she begins sculpting. However, as her dolls take shape, they begin "talking" to her. "Dolls tell you what color wigs they want, what they want to hold, what they want to do, what they want to wear. It's unbelievable. They speak to you." This affinity she has with the dolls is, in part, what makes them so captivating.

Creedy's one-of-a-kind dolls are generally 28 inches high and sell for about $4,000 each; those she creates in small editions are priced at $1,000 to $3,000. More affordable are the porcelain dolls she designs for the Barton's Creek line by Gund; introduced in 2000, they are limited to editions of 500 each. Vinyl versions of her original dolls are also available; they were introduced late in 2001 by Walterhausen Puppenmanufaktur.

Anrita, 28 inches, porcelain

Lucille III, 28 inches, porcelain

Heletta, 28 inches, porcelain

Paul Crees & Peter Coe

Since 1978, Paul Crees and Peter Coe have been making and selling some of the world's most hauntingly lovely dolls. Their entry into dollmaking began when Crees had to make a life-size figure of the Madonna for a play at England's famed Old Vic theater, where he was working as a set and costume designer. "The play bombed at the box office, but my Madonna statue got rave reviews," says Crees, who had made it out of Styrofoam. "I have had a lifelong fascination with Marlene Dietrich, so I used the same technique of construction and design to create a number of Dietrich figures. Peter was so impressed, he sold all of these one-of-a-kind figures to an art gallery."

After creating a few other characters, the men decided to reproduce their work in wax. "In this medium we were entirely self taught. I used to collect Peggy Nisbet dolls as a child and simply adored them. At that time, they were beautifully crafted. Her work was an early inspiration," says Crees, who was born in Bury, raised in Bristol, and studied set and costume design at Mountview Drama School in London. "Coincidentally, Peggy Nisbet was based in Weston Super Mare, where we now live, so life has turned a natural full circle," he adds.

Coe was born and raised in London. He enjoyed painting in his youth, and went on to study art at Ealing Technical College. However, he credits Crees with teaching him "everything I know about sculpting. We then worked together reviving and developing the Victorian wax medium for reproducing our work. It was an exciting phase of our lives." Crees and Coe developed their own formula for a durable and flexible wax, and they are the only artists in the world to create marbled-wax and two-tone wax sculptures.

Crees' and Coe's backgrounds in art and costume design are perfectly paired for the creation of dolls, especially as they approach it, which is to marry "the art of classic doll construction with sculpture cross-over techniques. We actually sculpt the whole figure, which is a very demanding process. With each doll, we strive to capture a moment in time. There must be drama in a piece, as well as a beautiful rendition of the subject. For a creation to work well, even the costume must convey a representation of historical accuracy as well as well-executed craftsmanship. You must know what you want to achieve in a doll sculpture. Every piece must convey your message of interpretation. Collectors want to own a piece of you, as well as a treasured work of your art. We always feel very privileged to know something we have created gives pleasure and happiness."

In recent years, Crees and Coe have also issued porcelain and vinyl versions of their designs. In 2001, they reduced the number of new designs they create annually for limited-edition production from sixteen to four, but they continue to do additional one-of-a-kind pieces. They've cut back on their dollmaking to concentrate on charity commitments. In 2001, for instance, they created a series of Princess Diana dolls to benefit The Pink Ribbons Crusade, a Texas-based breast cancer charity. "Having spent many years perfecting our craft and promoting the world of doll art through our Santa Fe Doll Art Show and other events, we feel we have reached a stage in our lives to make some positive returns to the community that will have lasting benefits," they say.

Princess Diana (White House), 28 inches, poured wax

Lady With a Parrot, 28 inches, poured wax

Emily in Blue, 28 inches, poured wax

I am very excited when I am designing and creating dolls," says Edna Dali, "but I also discovered that the creative work provides me with a kind of mental and emotional relaxation. I simply feel good when I sculpt, and I love it." The artists admits that she has a "hidden desire to always be creating something new, by myself," but it was the desire to be home with her three children during their formative years that "provided me with the strength to overcome all the difficulties and the obstacles I faced when I began making dolls, and to continue in my sculpting work."

Dali was born in Israel and earned a B.A. from Ben-Gurion University in Beer-Sheave, where she majored in geography and education. She later took courses in criminology in Israel and in art in England, where she and her husband lived for several years in the late 1970s. Then, in 1981, the Dalis moved to the United States, settling in Boston.

"My three children were small—just one, three and six years old—when I happened to meet Avigail Brahms. When I saw her dolls, I was fascinated by their beauty. I worked with her for a year, and at the same time took more art, sculpting and history courses." Dali then began sculpting dolls on her own, creating one-of-a-kinds from Fimo.

Always experimenting, going new directions, Dali has also created porcelain, resin and wax-over-porcelain dolls. "I do many types and varieties of dolls," says the artist. "They are different in age, looks, style, characters, size, pose. I make girls, boys, ladies, brides, character dolls, angels, heirloom dolls and dolls based on stories." She creates her own one-of-a-kind and limited-edition designs, as well as designs for other companies. In 1995, she began working with Seymour Mann, Inc., of New York City, which issues porcelain editions of her dolls in the United States. In 1997, she created dolls for Alberon Designs, for distribution in the United Kingdom. She also designs interactive toys for the Israeli Snubelgrass company.

Once again living in her native country, Dali is now entering her third decade as a dollmaker, and she is just as excited about her work and full of ideas as she was in the early 1980s. "Fashions, people and events of the past centuries provide me with a rich source of inspiration. I love to dress my dolls in real antique fabrics and styles, and I always add accessories to my dolls that make them authentic, real," says the artist, who scours antique stores and flea markets around the world for fabrics and accessories. *Victorian Lady*, for instance, is dressed in antique brocade and lace, with an elaborate floral headpiece and handmade leather shoes. This 29-inch, wax-over-porcelain doll has a dreamy, romantic look that is found in many of Dali's designs.

Dali's one-of-a-kind dolls sell for $1,200 to $6,000; her editions, usually limited to ten pieces, are priced between $800 and $2,500. "When I work with porcelain or wax-over-porcelain, I do about twenty-five designs a year. When I work with Fimo only, I make about fifteen dolls a year," she says. While she cites sculpting as the most challenging aspect of her artistry, what brings her great pleasure is contact with her collectors, who provide the impetus for her to continue to push the envelope on the art of dolls.

Victorian Lady, 29 inches, wax-over-porcelain

Girl Holding Doll, 20 inches, porcelain

The Juggler, 26 inches, white clay

*A*s the youngest of four children, Eileen De Vito was used to hand-me-downs. She didn't mind wearing her older sisters' outgrown clothing, but when it came to Christmas, she expected something nice of her very own. So each year, when her aunt would send dolls for the girls, she would be hopeful, but each year was the same. "At the top of the box would be a present for Mary. She was a blue-eyed blond, and she always received a blond doll with big blue eyes and a matching blue dress. Then there was a present for my sister Lily. She was a real Irish beauty, with long black hair and blue eyes, and she always got a doll with beautiful dark hair and a pretty pink dress. At the bottom of the box would be a rubber baby doll in a diaper—not even a dress—and it was for me." De Vito laughs as she tells this story, because the dolls she makes today are the exact opposite of those disappointing diapered dolls of her youth.

Born and raised in Bayside, New York, De Vito was always drawing or carving something as a child, until she began sewing at the age of ten. "I'd asked my mother if she would make a special dress for me to wear to my school's Snowball Dance. Instead, she took me to the old Grant's Department Story in Flushing, bought three yards of fabric for a dollar and handed it to me, saying, 'Let's see what you can do.'" De Vito not only made a dress out of those three yards of fabric, but also discovered a talent that she really enjoyed. It was several decades, however, before her sewing was anything more than a pleasant pastime.

"In 1980, after I'd had a serious operation, one of my sisters came to stay with me. On my sofa beside me was an antique reproduction of a Baby Hilda doll, a gift from my husband that I loved. After looking at it, my sister asked me, 'Why couldn't you do this? After all, you used to paint, you're a former beautician, and you can sew everything!' And that was the beginning of my journey into dollmaking," says De Vito.

After a few classes, she began making reproductions of antique dolls, for which she'd design vintage costumes. By 1984, she was selling her reproductions. A year later, she added reproductions of mechanical dolls to her repertoire. Finally, at the urging of friends, she signed up for a sculpting seminar given by Hildegard Günzel. "I've always loved and admired Hildegard's dolls, so you can imagine how embarrassed I was when I discovered that I was the only person in the seminar who had never, ever sculpted." Günzel didn't mind, though, and De Vito's years of carving as a kid, and experience in making reproductions of antique dolls stood her in good stead. By 1990 she was making and selling her own original dolls.

"I love every aspect of dollmaking: sculpting, painting and costuming. I design and complete all of the work myself, so my editions are small and the number of new dolls I design is limited," says De Vito. Most of her dolls depict women between the ages of eighteen and twenty-five. These lovely ladies, standing between 23 and 36 inches high, are the perfect models for De Vito's lavish costumes. Made from antique silks and satins, luxurious velvets, hand-beaded lace and other rich fabrics, the costumes make her creations dolls of distinction.

Midori, 23 inches, wax-over-porcelain

Peggy Dey

I grew up on a dairy farm in Central City, Nebraska, the youngest of eight children," says Peggy Dey. "Because we lived on a farm with few close neighbors, there weren't many opportunities to play with kids after school or on weekends. My brothers and sisters were all quite a bit older than I was, so animals and dolls were my playmates." One of her favorite early dolls was a Joanie Palooka, which was introduced when Dey was about a year old. "I still have her," the artist says, "although her head is now on a hard-plastic body, since I wore out several 'magic-skin' bodies before they were discontinued." Another favorite was a Patty Play Pal doll, which she purchased for herself at age nine with the $24.95 she saved from money her dad would give her for lunch.

As she matured, her dolls were put away and she concentrated on her studies. Dey earned a B.S. degree in psychology and an M.S. in clinical psychology from Fort Hays State University, Hays, Kansas, and has done extensive postgraduate work in school psychology at Fort Hays and the University of Kansas. After serving for two years at a community mental health clinic, Dey began working as a school psychologist, a profession she's pursued for more than twenty-five years.

Never having taken any art courses, and happy in her chosen career, Dey doubts that she would be making dolls today had she not fallen in love with Boots Tyner's *Sugar Britches*. "As a single mom of three," she says, "I couldn't afford to buy one. But someone suggested I could make one, so I decided to give it a try." She made her first reproduction doll in 1987. Two years later, she attended a sculpting seminar with Hildegard Günzel, and she's been creating her own dolls ever since. "I love the creative process, from sculpting the head to designing the costume," says Dey, who enjoys capturing a special moment in childhood with her pieces. Her specialty is young children between the ages of three and eight. "I think this is an age of wonder and innocence, an age when children are so open and uninhibited. I hope when people see my dolls, they evoke happy memories of the person's own childhood."

Dey began selling her dolls in 1991, and by 1992 knew she wanted to devote more time to her art. She arranged to work half time for the Lawrence, Kansas, school district, which she continues to do. Also, she was able to take a two-year leave of absence in the late 1990s. These steps provided needed time for her dollmaking, and freed her to attend some major doll shows, meet collectors and forge strong friendships with other doll artists. The number of dolls she sculpts annually varies from as few as four to as many as fifteen. She creates an occasional one-of-a-kind, generally priced at $2,000. She releases her vinyl editions, limited to between 100 and 300 pieces, under the name Heavenly Treasures; *Logan* is a typical example of her delightful vinyls. She also creates her own porcelain pieces, limited to editions of five to twenty-five, under the name Timeless Treasures. Some of Dey's family help out with her dolls, but she does the giant's share of the work on both the vinyls and porcelains by herself. Over the years, Dey has designed for other companies, including Hamilton Collection, The Danbury Mint, Effanbee and Ganz; all of them have issued porcelain editions of her creations.

Logan, 25 inches, vinyl

Val Ellick

I started collecting dolls many years ago, after my husband Greg gave me a doll for Christmas. This led me to reproduction dollmaking, but copying other people's work was not for me, so I started looking for information on creating my own dolls. I found a wonderful teacher, and have been selling my dolls since 1994," says Val Ellick, who was born in England, but has lived in Australia since she was sixteen. Her dolls have won awards at many Australian shows, and have been honored in America as nominees for *Dolls* magazine's Awards of Excellence and *Doll Reader*'s Doll of the Year (DOTY) awards.

The vast majority of Ellick's dolls are porcelain, although recently she's made some molded-face cloth pieces. "Some people say my dolls have an English look. Maybe you can never completely get away from your roots," muses the artist. "My dolls depict young children—I love the sweet innocence of youth—and I am beginning to do some work on Australian aboriginal children."

Twenty-eight-inch *Laura* is typical of Ellick's porcelain dolls, most of which are between 22 and 28 inches high. *Laura*'s head, arms and legs are porcelain; its body is made from calico, with Lycra "skin." The doll has soft-glass eyes and a mohair wig. *Laura*'s dress showcases the artist's love for intricate handwork. "I was close to my two grandmothers, who passed on their talents in needlework and handwork, skills that seem to be lost in today's world," says Ellick, who believes that costuming is extremely important in the overall look of a doll. She loves to do the smocking, pleating, embroidery and other fancy needlework that have become trademarks of her dolls.

It's not just the costuming that Ellick does by herself. Her dolls, whether one-of-a-kinds or limited editions, are completely created by the artist only. She even makes her own molds and wigs. Because dolls are such a labor-intensive art form, she sculpts just four to six new designs each year. Generally, three of these are issued in limited editions of twenty pieces, and the others are one-of-a-kinds. Her limited-edition pieces sell for between $800 and $1,800 each; prices for her one-of-a-kinds begin around $2,000.

In addition to making dolls, Ellick now teaches dollmaking. Also, she continues to collect dolls, buying the work of other artists whom she admires, as she never seems able to keep any of her own. Since the latter part of the 1990s, when Ellick first showed her dolls at the American International Toy Fair, an annual trade show held in New York City, the demand for her dolls has outstripped her ability to create them. The artist, however, continues to attend shows in the United States annually. Her husband often accompanies her to these shows, now that their four sons have grown up and left home.

While many artists find traveling around the world to exhibit their dolls one of the few perks of their profession, Ellick ("a very private person—some would say a little reclusive," she admits) finds joy in the solitude of working all day in her studio, with just her poodles, Sammy and Zoe, for company. "There is no better feeling," she says, "than seeing a finished doll, having watched it evolve from a block of clay."

Laura, 28 inches, porcelain

Yvonne Flipse

In the late 1970s, Yvonne Flipse attended a show in Belgium at which artist dolls were featured, and she thought, "I can do that also." And she was right, even though she had never previously done any sculpting and had no formal art training. However, the artist—who was born in Goes, The Netherlands, and raised in Krabbendijke—had enjoyed drawing and painting as a child, and she liked playing with dolls, especially Barbie. But unlike many of today's top doll artists, Flipse had had no interest in making clothing for her childhood playthings, although she did enjoy cutting their hair, "which made my mother very angry," she recalls.

After selling her first doll in 1978, Flipse began showing her work throughout Europe. By the early 1990s, she was winning major European awards: Germany's 1991 Euro Doll Gold, and Euro Doll Top Best awards in 1992, 1993 and 1994. In 1994, she also won a Global Doll Best Doll award in England. Then in 1995, she was honored with Germany's Glaserner Feenstrab award. Americans finally got a chance to see her work in 1996, when she attended the Santa Fe Doll Art Show organized by Paul Crees and Peter Coe. The following year, she participated in the Masterpieces of the World exhibition in New York City, organized by Sonja Hartmann. She has also participated in exhibitions in Peru, Canada, Japan and Russia. She began the new millennium by winning the Best Original Doll award in a Moscow competition.

Flipse works with Paperclay and creates one-of-a-kinds only, making about twenty a year. They range from about 10 to 21 inches in height. Prices for them begin around $1,000 and go to more than $6,000. Her dolls are very sculptural—on the borderline of what might be defined as a doll. Most of her pieces are slim, stylized figures of delicate young women, although she does some male figures, too. Pieces may be wigged, or they may have papier-mâché hair. Their costumes are often a combination of fabric and clay. "I put my feelings in my creations. I work with my heart and soul," says Flipse. "I love nature, the sky, the moon, the flowers, watercolors, antiques, music, dancing, emotions—that is also what I put in the dolls." *Ballerina*, shown here, is a typical example of her work. The seated, ten-inch doll is sculpted completely from Paperclay and has been painted by Flipse with watercolors. She has crafted a mohair wig for the doll, and used clay and fabric to fashion the costume. While the dancer is shown in repose, there is a grace and fluidity in this piece that is found in the majority of Flipse's dolls.

"I think the most important thing in my life is to have fun in my work, and it is also lovely that other people love my dolls and have the same feelings about them that I do," says Flipse. She gets great pleasure out of the entire dollmaking process, and also enjoys the travel and the friends she's met through her art. While her husband, Emiel Hoogesteger, is supportive of her art, her son scoffs at her dolls. Her daughter, on the other hand, would like to keep them all, as would her many collectors.

Ballerina, 10 inches, Paperclay

Tom Francirek & Andre Oliveira

Wax dollmaking reached its heights in England after Anna Marie Tussaud opened her famed wax museum in London in the early 1800s. The museum featured life-size models that charmed England's aristocrats and commoners alike, and no doubt stimulated interest in the wax dolls being made at the time by the Pierotti and Montanari families. It is appropriate, then, that Tom Francirek—one of the few dollmakers today who, with his partner, Andre Oliveira, uses wax as one of his media—began his career as the manager of a Tussaud's wax museum. Francirek quickly became fascinated by the museum's figures and began creating lobby displays for the various holidays by reworking and re-costuming them. He enjoyed the creative work much more than the managerial portion of his job, and had exhibited a flair for it, so asked if he could do other artistic projects. Within a year, Francirek was head of Tussaud's art department. While he created life-size figures at work, he began making miniature wax sculptures—poured-wax dolls—in his free time. In 1991, he began selling his dolls.

Oliveira had a more traditional art background. He had been painting and drawing since childhood, and, he says, "pursued an academic career in the arts at a university

 level." He created mixed-media works, but was happiest depicting the human form. When he and Francirek became friends, they discovered a shared interest in wax dollmaking; Oliveira was initially Francirek's assistant, but eventually they formed a creative partnership.

Today, Francirek and Oliveira create lovely poured-wax and porcelain dolls that are issued jointly under their names. Their one-of-a-kinds are wax and sell for $4,500 to $8,000 each; their porcelain dolls are issued in editions of ten to fifteen pieces. *Laura* is a typical example of their porcelain work, which weds finely detailed sculpting with adroit costuming. "Hopefully, our love for all things beautiful shines through in all aspects of our dolls," says Oliveira. "We strive to create a magic with the costuming, painting and movement."

The artists claim no preference for ethnicity or age group, but admit that they "love creating romantic and sensual lady dolls. Their creation can be incredibly involving, but they communicate on many different levels. We find people respond to our lady dolls from their own personal perspectives. Little girls see the fantasy of adulthood, or perhaps fairy tale princesses; women see ladies from eras inhabited by romance; and men see an almost unattainable, sensually innocent object of desire. Yet," they add, "there is nothing more satisfying than capturing the innocence of childhood through the creation of a doll."

Both Francirek and Oliveira were born in Ontario and are first-generation Canadians. Francirek's parents emigrated from Prague, Czechoslovakia. Oliveira's parents came from the Azores. Their families taught them a love and respect for European art and culture, which has influenced their lives and their work. Like other male dollmakers, they enjoy the technical aspects of dollmaking, but say that it is "the incredible freedom given us as artists to explore that is truly the most enjoyable aspect of dollmaking—whether it be through clay in the sculpting process, or through color and fabric layering in the costuming process." One can only hope that these young men—both are in their early thirties—will continue to be challenged by the art form and to lend their considerable talents to it for many years to come.

Laura, 28 inches seated, porcelain

I have always loved dolls and have been making them in various ways since childhood," says Elissa Glassgold, who was born and raised in Detroit, Michigan. "I didn't realize that there could be a profession related to this until I saw Annette Himstedt's first vinyl dolls at F.A.O. Schwarz. I think a light bulb went on in my head that day, and I realized that I wanted to be a doll artist."

Although making dolls as a career was not a childhood dream, even as a youngster Glassgold knew her future was in the arts. "My parents were both artists and always encouraged me to pursue my love of drawing and painting," she says. "They are deceased, and never knew that I became a doll designer/artist, but I am sure they would have loved my work. I think that like most artists, making the decision to pursue art was not really a 'decision' as much as a realization of identity. I don't think I ever considered any other path."

Upon graduating from high school, Glassgold attended the Pennsylvania Academy of the Fine Arts, where she was awarded two European study tours. She then earned a Bachelor of Fine Arts degree and a Master of Art Education from the University of Arts/Philadelphia, and a Master of Fine Arts from the University of North Carolina. From 1987 to 1996, she was a professor of painting and art history at Rutgers-Temple Universities and at the Hudsian School of Art in Philadelphia. She is married and has a son, Nathaniel.

Glassgold began making dolls in 1988 and sold her first doll the following year. She continues to do traditional painting and sculpting, but notes that the sculpting and painting of dolls has special appeal because "dolls reach people in a unique way. They are historically significant in that they are a very ancient and ongoing art form that provides people with a great deal of comfort and hope. They hold memories and sentiment for many people," she says, adding, "My own dolls from childhood were very important for me, and I wanted to create a series of new dolls that might have that power for their collectors."

The artist prefers to use "earth clay" for sculpting, but loves the look of Fimo and Cernit, which she uses for her one-of-a-kinds. She makes about ten one-of-a-kinds each year; they are generally 30 to 34 inches high and sell for $2,500 to $4,000 each. She also creates limited-edition dolls, generally limited to three to twenty pieces; they cost between $750 and $3,000. Since 1999, she has been designing two to three dolls a year for Zapf Creations, which reproduces them in vinyl.

Most of Glassglod's dolls depict children between the ages of seven and nine, though she has created a few dolls of babies. "I have enjoyed most creating Asian and African-American children," she notes. "I grew up in a very diverse area, and am very observant of faces. They seem to emerge on their own from the clay." It is the "point when a face suddenly becomes who it is going to be" that she most enjoys when making a doll; however, she admits that sculpting is also the most challenging part of dollmaking. "I am trained as a painter, so seeing things three-dimensionally is quite difficult for me. Getting the work to be correct from every angle is quite a challenge."

One need only look at Glassgold's creations to see it's a challenge she has mastered.

Maidie and *Gwen*, each 30 inches, vinyl

Miss Magrit's Daughter, Orlando—the Ambassador's Child, Cleofé, each 34 inches, cast resin

Julie Good-Krüger

*A*s a child, I collected antique dolls with my grandmother. I wrote stories about my dolls and made clothing for them. After graduating from college, I had a dream one night where I saw myself making dolls, and I simply decided to do it," says Julie Good-Krüger, who was born and raised in Berlin, Wisconsin, and had planned to be an archeology professor. She attended St. Olaf College in Northfield, Minnesota, where she studied classics and ancient history, and spent two years studying the classics at England's Oxford University. Later, she attended some life sculpture seminars at the Scottsdale Artist School in Arizona and had private tutorials in art.

After her dollmaking dream, Good-Krüger began to sculpt. Initially, she saw doll-making as a way to earn money for graduate school, but later, she says, "it just absorbed my interest." Of course, in order to create porcelain dolls, she had to learn mold making,

the ins and outs of kiln firing, how to set dolls' eyes, and the best methods for painting porcelain. She spent several years experimenting with various media, mastering the skills needed for each, and developing ideas for her dolls and their costumes. Then she began making one-of-a-kind and limited-edition porcelain dolls. Helping her through her difficult time of experimentation was a fellow St. Olaf graduate, Tim Krüger; by the time she was satisfied with her dolls, he was her husband and partner in Good-Krüger Dolls.

Good-Krüger sold her first dolls in 1981, and quickly attracted attention among doll collectors. As the demand for her dolls grew, she began issuing vinyl editions, which were equally embraced by her collectors. In 1991 she also began doing some designs for The Ashton-Drake Galleries; in all, she's designed nearly fifty dolls for the Niles, Illinois, company. In the late 1990s, she began working for The Boyds Collection Ltd. Today, she is Boyds' head doll designer, and as such she designed the company's complete 2000 and 2001 doll collections. When she began working for Boyds, the couple closed their own doll company, and Tim began taking classes at a Lutheran seminary; he also does some consulting in the collectibles world and emergency substitute teaching for schools in their area of Pennsylvania.

In addition to creating dolls, Good-Krüger does some architectural ceramics and relief sculpture. She also enjoys drawing, creative writing and playing the piano. "It just happened that I focused on dolls, probably because in the making of a doll, many of my interests can be integrated: sculpture, painting, fiber arts, doll collecting and storytelling," says Good-Krüger, whose dolls depicting children, usually under the age of ten, have been nominated for and received many prestigious awards. "I like to sculpt children as dolls because of the opportunities for clothing and gesture and storytelling," says the artist. "When I do straight sculpture, like busts, I prefer to sculpt old people, because so much can be said with just the face and the tilt of the head."

Megan and Faithful...Old and Dear Friends is typical of Good-Krüger's work. Designed for The Boyds Collection Ltd., the 12-inch doll wears a hand-embroidered cotton dress over a slip and pantaloons; on her feet are resin shoes. In her arms is her first teddy bear, also from Boyds, of course.

Megan and Faithful...Old and Dear Friends, 12 inches, porcelain and resin

*F*ew artists have had more influence on the world of dolls than Hildegard Günzel. Born in Germany's romantic, 1,200-year-old city of Tauberbischhofsheim, she attended the German Master School for Fashion and Design and, after graduation, worked as a fashion and jewelry designer until she began making dolls in 1972. "The first doll I created was for my son Kai, when he was one year old. This doll was a little bit ugly. As a professional designer, I wanted my three-dimensional work to be as good as my two-dimensional designs. At that time, there was nobody to learn from, so it was really learning by doing." Five years later, in 1977, she sold her first doll.

The world of contemporary art dolls was still in its infancy when, in the early 1980s, Günzel joined forces with Mathias Wanke, of M. Wanke GmbH, allowing him to issue molds of her dolls so hobbyists could reproduce them. Until then, Wanke distributed materials and offered classes for reproducing antique dolls only. Wanke sold dollmaking

supplies around the world, and the beauty of Günzel's contemporary designs inspired many ceramic hobbyists to embrace dollmaking. Some of them, such as New Zealand's Jan McLean, went on to become world-renowned dollmakers. Molds of Günzel's designs are no longer available; however, the artist still shares her knowledge of dollmaking through books she's published about her techniques. She has also produced a video titled "Modelling with Hildegard Günzel."

Günzel began sculpting her originals in Cernit, but today prefers plasti-line. Her finished dolls, however, are all porcelain—and since the early 1980s, she has been covering them with a special wax that gives them a mar-velous translucency. She makes one-of-a-kind dolls, which sell for $15,000 to $40,000 each, and issues wax-over-porcelain editions limited to twenty-five pieces for United States dis-tribution and twenty-five for Europe. They are made at her company, House of Günzel, in Duisburg, Germany; prices for them begin around $5,000. She has designed dolls for Walterhauser Puppenmanufaktur, which has produced them in Biggidur. Also, in 2000, she designed a line of play dolls for Götz, and in 2001, she began designing collector dolls for Götz to issue in vinyl.

Although Günzel has won countless awards for her dolls, she is not one to rest on her laurels. "I'm developing my techniques every time I make a doll, and I will never stop learning," she says. She also enjoys trying new things. For instance, in 1996 she turned her talents to creating teddy bears. They were such a success that she founded Hildegard Günzel Teddybär GmbH to produce them. That same year, she opened a museum adjacent to her studio; named The Museum for Contemporary Doll Art, it displays many of Günzel's dolls and busts, as well as other artists' dolls from her personal collection. These include examples by Annette Himstedt, Brigitte Deval, and Steve and Angela Clark.

Günzel delights in surprising her collectors, and each of her creations is completely new and different. If there is anything that can be said to be typical about them, it is that they are all extremely realistic and exquisitely crafted, from the smoothness of the porcelain and its wax covering to the beautifully designed and constructed cos-tumes. "My goal," she says, "is to use only the best." This, coupled with her innate talent and impeccable taste, make her dolls true works of art.

Celestine, 31 inches, wax-over-porcelain

Gwendolyn, 33 inches, wax-over-porcelain

Vinette, 33 inches, wax-over-porcelain

When she was in her thirties, Ella Hass developed an interest in antique dolls and began collecting them. As her exposure to dolls and her knowledge of them grew, so did a desire to make her very own. She began to do so in 1984, and felt confident enough about her work to sell her first doll in 1986. The chief inspiration for her early pieces was the work of German dollmaker Kathe Krüse (1883-1968). "Her technique had a tremendous appeal for me," says Hass, who developed her own unique methods for making cloth dolls after repairing a Kathe Krüse doll and talking with Krüse's daughter, Fifi.

Each of this Danish dollmaker's pieces begins with a sculpture of the doll's head, in clay or Plastilina. She then makes a mold of the head, and uses it to create a head in Keramin, a durable, plaster-like material made in Germany. Next, she coats the Keramin head with wax and applies a tricot mask. After priming the mask, Hass paints the doll's

face with oil paints. The bodies of her dolls are made of fabric and have metal armatures; their arms and legs are composition. The limbs, she says, "are cast in molds made of a sort of plaster-clay."

Hass creates one-of-a-kind and limited-edition dolls, but her editions never exceed six pieces. Because of her time-consuming process, she is able to make only ten or twelve dolls a year; prices for them begin around $6,500. "I like small children, and I only make dolls as one- to six-year-olds," says Hass, who has four children of her own, all now grown. Most of her dolls have a pouty, pensive look, and are about 27 inches high. They have either mohair or human-hair wigs, and wear outfits designed by the artist and made from natural fabrics, such as wool and cotton.

Born and raised in Esbjerg, Denmark, Hass is truly a self-taught artist. As a child, she dreamed of being a nurse, and did volunteer work in a hospital after school. Unfortunately, allergies—including allergies to ingredients used in soap—made a medical career impossible, so she went into teaching. Because of the success of her dolls, today Hass is a "full-time dollmaker."

One year after she sold her first doll, Hass received a gold medal for her work from the Global Doll Society. The following year, *Cieslik's Puppen Magazin* of Germany featured her work. Since then, she has been featured in a number of European and American magazines, and the excellence of her work has been further recognized by two Max-Oscar-Arnold-Kunstpreis awards. Her dolls have been featured in exhibits throughout Europe, in Japan and the United States, and in 1999, Hass was elected into the National Institute of American Doll Artists.

Hass says that her motto is, "One sees and feels if a doll is made with an honest heart—like art in general." Her dolls, such as *Philippa* and *Sarah*, are proof of her honest heart. They are typical examples of her sweet portraits of children contemplating the world around them.

Philippa and *Sarah*, each 27 inches, Keramin

*J*oëlle Lemasson, who is known in the art world by the name Héloïse, may not have been the first dollmaker to use resin, but she was surely the first to make such exquisite use of it. She chose it as her medium back in 1982, when not only were there few artists making dolls, but those who were reproduced their designs almost exclusively in porcelain. Héloïse dared to be different and developed a special formula for her resin, which is tinted throughout, resulting in a look that closely resembles skin. She then began creating aesthetic portraits of children and young ladies—dolls skillfully sculpted, delicately painted and costumed to perfection. Today, she creates dolls primarily representing French children, although she did introduce a Creole child in her 2001 line. While the artist describes them as "both modern and romantic," they have a timeless quality that lets the viewer imagine them existing in almost any century of the past or future.

All of Héloïse's dolls have resin heads, shoulder plates, hands and feet; some, however, also have resin bodies, and creating them, she says, is her biggest challenge. "To realize a doll entirely in resin is very difficult, because each part of the doll has to be made separately and jointed." The success she has with this can be seen in *Paule*, a 19-inch doll with painted features and a mohair wig. It was created in 2001 and limited to an edition of thirty-five.

Héloïse was born and raised in Saint Malo, France. She is a graduate of the Ecole Des Beaux Arts de Rennes, where she studied to be an art teacher. She has created paintings and traditional sculptures, which she still does, but says, "I feel closer to doll sculpting. It is more emotional." She began making rag dolls in 1976, initially as playthings for her two young children, but later for sale in French stores. Her love of sculpting drove her to look for a medium in which to reproduce her original clay sculptures, of which she makes three or four a year. She issues her dolls in limited editions of up to fifty pieces. "Each piece in the edition has been painted by me as a unique doll," says Héloïse, who also tends to do additional modeling on her dolls after they are removed from the mold. Changes to the area around the eyes and to the lips give each doll its unique personality, as do different wigs and costumes.

The artist first showed her resin dolls in Paris, at the 1982 "Atelier d'Art Show," where they earned raves from fellow artists. Three years and a number of exhibits later, the Musée des Arts Décoratifs in Paris purchased one of her dolls for its permanent collection. More major French exhibits followed, but Héloïse's dolls were not well known outside of France until 1989, when she first showed them in the United States. Her dolls were enthusiastically embraced by American collectors, and Héloïse continues to have a dedicated following here, as well as in Europe. She is a founding member of the Association Française de Poupées D'Artists and has been honored with many awards, including the 1994 Jumeau Trophee award and the 1994 Global Doll Society's top award in the new medium category.

Paule, 19 inches, resin

Josephine, 20 inches, resin

Paule (another version), 19 inches, resin

*C*oming across one of her mother's childhood dolls during a closet-cleaning session sparked Margie Herrara's interest in dolls—an interest that grew into a passion for creating her own original designs. "Mom's old doll was in need of repair, so I took her to a doll hospital. When we got her back, I fell in love with her. I began reading about old dolls, then about new artists' dolls. Then I came across a book by Hildegard Günzel on dollmaking, and it inspired me to start working with porcelain."

With Günzel's book on how to sculpt as her bible ("I've referred to it so often that it's tattered and worn," she says) and the added help of Mary Yap, who makes reproductions from molds of Hawaiian dolls, Herrera learned the basics of porcelain dollmaking. She then began to experiment, honing her skills by trial and error. "In her book, Hildegard stresses that you should always challenge yourself to do better," notes Herrera, who lives by that sage advice. In 1996, more than two decades after falling in love with her mother's old doll, Herrera began selling her own designs.

"Most of my dolls depict young ladies—teenagers," says the artist, who was born in California, but has lived mostly in Hawaii since 1973. "I like the fashions I can create for more adult dolls, rather than children, but I always want them to be sweet, to represent the beauty of girls on the brink of womanhood. I love elegant gowns, and since we don't wear them often now, I enjoy making dolls that can wear them as often as they like. I also love making bridal gowns for my creations."

Herrera's work has been featured in national doll magazines, but her name is not widely known. That's due, in part, to the limited availability of her designs. There are no doll shops on the island of Maui, where she and her husband Carlos live, and the stores that do carry dolls limit them to Hawaiian designs for tourists, she explains. Also, she is reluctant to ask people to pay for her art. Consequently, she continues to hold a full-time job, working on her dolls during the evenings, late at night, and in the early mornings. She sculpts about four dolls a year, creating an occasional one-of-a-kind, but mostly making them in editions of up to twenty pieces.

Typical of Herrera's designs is 28-inch *Ruby*, which is costumed in an 1880s-style ball gown. Its head, arms and legs are porcelain; its body is cloth over an armature. Most of Herrera's dolls are 26 to 35 inches high, but she is beginning to work on some smaller, 18- to 20-inch designs. She is also experimenting with some all-porcelain pieces.

Herrera says her house is "full of dolls," but fortunately her husband is very supportive of her artistry. Their three adopted children—all now adults and living in their own homes on the island of Maui—also think her dolls are great, she says, but they tend to tease her each time she begins a new design. She has no plans of stopping, though. "I get a really great feeling when I sculpt," she says. "I would have a difficult time putting the clay down. If I were able, I would make dolls that evoke the beauty and values of each young person, of every race, male and female. I'm always trying to expand, to be better and do more," she adds.

Ruby, 28 inches, porcelain

nnette Himstedt sculpts sweet, realistic children and delights in making up stories about them—stories that are much happier than the artist's own youth. By the time she was a teenager, Himstedt, who was born in Anhalt, Germany, had moved with her family thirteen times, including escaping from East Germany just before the Berlin Wall was built. Because of this constant uprooting, Himstedt had few childhood friends, so took comfort in drawing and reading. In West Germany, her family suffered financial difficulties, acerbated by the death of her father when she was eleven years old. Himstedt showed promise as an artist, but there was no money for lessons or advanced education.

Married at an early age, Himstedt had her first child, Dierk, when she was eighteen years old; her daughter, Imke, was born thirteen months later. In 1974, wanting to create three-dimensional portraits of children, she began experimenting with dollmaking. "It

took me years until I managed to make a face that I was happy with—let alone a whole doll," says Himstedt. "I never really planned to model dolls at all, but it was the only way to make the 'person' complete. That's why I made my first Kinder aus Porzellan"—child of porcelain—a term she prefers to "doll." "I started making stone figures, then I sewed dolls made of fabric and ended up modeling dolls in clay. I soon became dissatisfied with clay as a material and investigated how to make dolls from porcelain," says the artist, who worked as a clothing model to support her dollmaking efforts. In 1979, she went to a nearby porcelain factory for advice, which was not forthcoming; but she was befriended by a mold maker, with whom she worked for about a dozen years.

Himstedt debuted her dolls at a 1982 Christmas exhibit in a Munich department store, where she made her first sale. Much hard work followed, but so did success. An article in a German magazine brought international attention to her portrait dolls of actual children, and she received a lot of commissions. She added vinyl dolls to her line, and from the mid 1980s to 1996, she had a contract with Mattel to distribute them in the United States. By 1990, she had built her own factory, and she now has a small staff working with her to produce her dolls, which are cherished by collectors around the world. *Jana*, introduced in 2001, is typical of her Puppen Kinder (vinyl) dolls.

"My specialty is that I not only design the dolls, but also produce them in the complete sense of the word, using the highest quality materials available. This includes the vinyl that I have perfected over many years and the use of the highest quality porcelain available. It continues through to the wigs, the accessories, the clothing and shoes that I design, and the fabrics that are exclusively made for me. I also enjoy being able to offer a wide range of unique dolls that collectors with different tastes can relate to. From the modern play dolls through to the realistic doll children and the exquisite porcelain editions, I try to create a beauty that will make an emotional connection with people," she says.

Himstedt's dolls depict children of all ages and nationalities. She sculpts seventeen to nineteen new dolls a year. Typically, three or four are for her Kinder aus Porzellan collection, and seven of them are for the Puppen Kinder collection. The others are Himies (play dolls) or Winzlinge (little dolls with carriages).

Jana, 32 inches, vinyl

Jantje and *Santje*, 26¾ and 28 inches, porcelain

Snowdrop Fairy, 26 inches, porcelain

I began tinkering with dollmaking in 1984, but it was not until 1991 that I began it as a full-time profession," says Maggie Iacono. Three years later, she was honored with membership in the National Institute of American Doll Artists. During her first decade of dollmaking, she won seven Awards of Excellence from *Dolls* magazine and three of *Doll Reader*'s DOTY awards. Her felt dolls are sold under the name Maggie Made in stores here and abroad, and are on permanent display in the Louvre Museum in Paris.

Iacono was born and raised in Minnesota. When she was eighteen, she moved with her parents to Utica, New York. She attended the State University of New York, Fredonia, and earned a B.A. degree in elementary education. She then went to Australia, where she taught school for two years. While there, she met Tony Iacono; they were married in 1976 and have three children.

The artist became interested in dolls after reading Kyoko Yoneyama's book titled *The Collection of Stuffed Dolls From a Fancy World*. "It outlined a technique of crafting cloth dolls that I found so fascinating I had to try it," says Iacono. As she worked on these dolls, she thought of them as a way to make money while home with her young children. But then she found other doll patterns to try, and before she knew it, she was "hooked. Gradually," she says, "I became confident enough to create my own original work."

Iacono's dolls may be made of fabric, but they begin with a clay sculpture. "I use Chavant, a type of plasticine clay, to work the original sculpture, and then further refine the sculpture in wax," explains the artist. "Through a series of molds, I come up with the 'pressing mold' that is used for the pressing of the felt for the face. The body is also made of felt." She creates about nine new dolls a year. Three of them are generally one-of-a-kinds, ranging in price from $2,000 to $3,500; the others are issued in limited editions of twenty to seventy-five pieces. The limited-edition dolls sell for $800 to $1,000. The majority depict children, such as *Petals*, one of her 17-inch dolls issued in 2001. "When designing, children have always popped quite naturally into my mind. I think it is their sweet innocence that attracts me, as well as the potential for more creative and fun costuming. I am currently, however, sculpting an adult figure. I am doing this to stretch and try new areas that may lead who knows where," says the artist.

A perfectionist, Iacono believes that when "creating a doll, you should be concerned with the total 'package.' By this I mean color, form, texture, quality in craftsmanship, and so forth. When these are put together well, you know you have something of beauty put before you. I combine these with a very unique medium and technique of pressing felt. I put a great deal of attention to the costuming of my dolls. I delight in coming up with special details that make the clothing unique." It is just such attention to detail, coupled with Iacono's never-ending quest for better ways to do things and constant striving to make each doll better than the last, that makes the artist and her dolls so very loved by collectors, and so respected by her peers.

Petals, 17 inches, cloth

Jessica, 17 inches, cloth

Willow, 17 inches, cloth

*I*t may not be surprising to learn that Hanna Kahl-Hyland's preferred medium is wood, since she was born and raised in Germany—a country with a long history of wood carving. What is surprising is that she makes wooden dolls, rather than nutcrackers and whirligigs, the traditional German decorations. But, then, Kahl-Hyland came to dollmaking quite by chance.

As a child, she enjoyed sketching and painting. Her mother, an artist and musician, encouraged her creativity. At age ten, Kahl-Hyland began taking private lessons in watercolor and oil painting; later, she took sculpture classes at a local art school. After her marriage, she moved to England and spent three years studying sculpture at London's St. Martin's School of Arts, where her aptitude for wood carving was recognized. In the mid 1970s, Kahl-Hyland moved to the United States; she and her husband settled in Connecticut, and she continued to hone her skills by studying painting at the Paier Art School in New Haven and portrait sculpture at the Lyme Academy in Old Lyme.

A magazine article on making apple-head dolls, which Kahl-Hyland came across in 1980, inspired her first dollmaking efforts. The project looked fun, and since she'd always loved fairy tales, she decided to make apple-head dolls of the Seven Dwarfs. She was pleased with the results, but decided she needed a Snow White to complete the scene, so she carved one from wood. Having enjoyed herself, she went on to create more scenes from fairy tales. Worried that apples would rot, she stuck with wood as her medium. About ten years later, a curator of the Pittsburgh Children's Museum came across her work, and mounted an exhibition of her fairy-tale dolls.

In 1991, Kahl-Hyland began selling her one-of-a-kind dolls; most are 20 to 30 inches high and sell for between $3,000 and $7,000. In 1992, she began creating designs for Seymour Mann, Inc., of New York City, which reproduces her work in porcelain. In 1993, she was commissioned to carve four fairy-tale dolls for a Tiffany's, Boston, window display. Since then, her dolls have been featured at a number of exhibitions and shows.

Kahl-Hyland has experimented with porcelain and Paperclay (and she's created some outstanding dolls in these media), but she finds herself constantly returning to wood and the special challenge it presents. "I think the one aspect of carving that is not really understood or appreciated is that mistakes cannot be rectified. Carving in wood or stone is a process of reduction; each cut is a definite decision," she notes. One slip of the chisel, or even a bit too much sanding, can ruin a doll and its tiny features. Although Kahl-Hyland grows very tense while carving, the successful completion of a piece is worth the effort.

At one time, she says, "I felt quite guilty about spending so much time on the creation of dolls, particularly when colleagues kept asking when I intended to start sculpting again." Now when friends say that, she explains that "the creation of a doll encompasses many aspects. There's the sculpting, the painting, the possibility of movement through jointing, and the ability to let fantasy reign when it comes to costuming." Kahl-Hyland, who carves just two to four dolls a year, brings great talent to each aspect. She gives the same attention to selecting the right wood for each creation, and finding the perfect vintage fabrics for their outfits, as she does to carving, jointing and painting.

Adrienne, 24 inches, bass wood

Violetta, 24 inches, cherry wood

Frog Prince, 27 inches, bass wood

*I*f curiosity could kill, Diane Keeler wouldn't have made it past childhood, for it has been the driving force of her life and one, she tells us, that her mother and father abetted. "When I was growing up, my parents were always doing something, always trying a new hobby or pursuing a new interest. They encouraged all five of us girls to do the same thing," says the Duluth, Minnesota, born and bred dollmaker.

After studying fashion design in vocational school, Keeler attended beauty school and then worked as a hairdresser for seventeen years. While it takes talent to cut and style hair, Keeler's real creativity went into the hobbies and craft projects that filled her free time. First there was sewing and furniture upholstery, then came weaving, spinning, knitting, basket making, quilting, leatherwork and jewelry making. Like her parents, she was

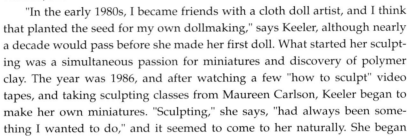

always trying something new; once she'd mastered it, or made what she wanted, she'd move on.

"In the early 1980s, I became friends with a cloth doll artist, and I think that planted the seed for my own dollmaking," says Keeler, although nearly a decade would pass before she made her first doll. What started her sculpting was a simultaneous passion for miniatures and discovery of polymer clay. The year was 1986, and after watching a few "how to sculpt" video tapes, and taking sculpting classes from Maureen Carlson, Keeler began to make her own miniatures. "Sculpting," she says, "had always been something I wanted to do," and it seemed to come to her naturally. She began exhibiting her miniature figures at shows and winning awards. By 1994, she had added dolls to her repertoire, and their success enabled her to become a full-time artist. "I get bored very easily," says Keeler, "but dollmaking keeps me excited." The most challenging aspect, she says, is "to evoke emotion in the hands, which are usually the very last things I do on a piece."

Keeler continues to use polymer clay for her sculptures. "I worked with them all, and then settled on a Cernit and Super Sculpey mix." She personally makes about twenty-five dolls a year, all one-of-a-kinds, plus she designs a line of dolls for the Home Shopping Network. "I do mainly children, approximately four to seven years old, but I like doing young girls just developing and women, too," says Keeler. Her seated dolls range in height from nine to 14 inches; her standing dolls are up to 20 inches high. Her dolls are very realistic, and just like real children, they display a variety of emotions, from thoughtful to joyous. *Mara*, a 12-inch seated doll, is typical of her work. Keeler was elected to membership in the prestigious National Institute of American Doll Artists (NIADA) in 2001.

While Keeler is dedicated to dollmaking, it's simply not in her nature to stick to just one thing for too long. So, she has added teaching dollmaking to her schedule. Among her special talents is wigging, blending clays and fine finishing. Also, with all her years of doing handicrafts and her early training in fashion design, she's great at costuming. The clothing she makes for her dolls is as varied as her interests, ranging from bibbed jeans to lace-trimmed Victorian-style day dresses, but always the perfect pick for the personality of the doll wearing it.

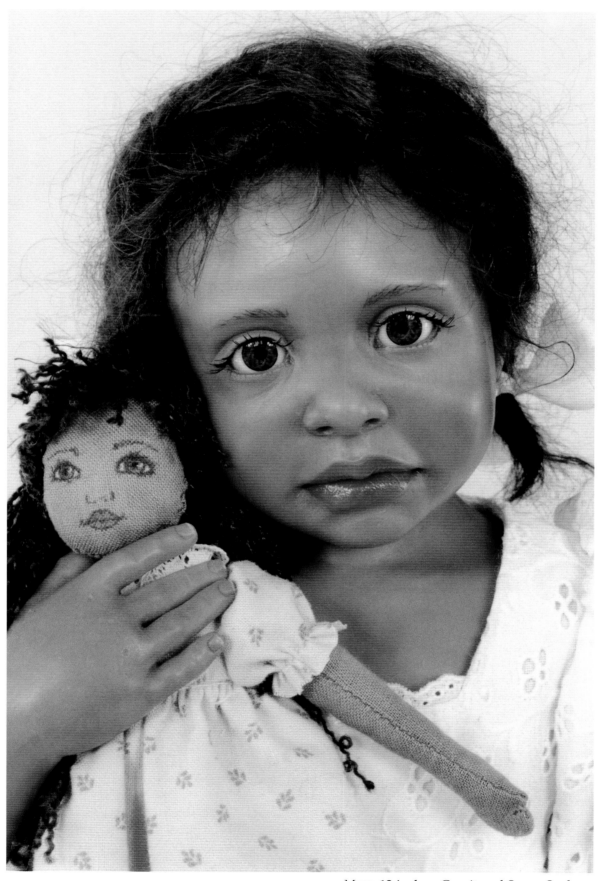

Mara, 12 inches, Cernit and Super Sculpey

*G*od gives us all gifts. It is up to us to take those gifts and develop them to the best of our ability. I have tried to do this," says Helen Cunalta Kish, whose beautiful dolls have captivated collectors for more than two decades. "It would have been so much easier for me and my family if I had had a regular nine-to-five job, with weekends off and a yearly vacation. But that wasn't to be. Sculpting and designing has been an all-consuming passion for me. That there are others who are touched by my work gives me the courage to keep on doing it."

Born and raised in Denver, Colorado, Kish began making paper dolls at age seven. "I listened to the grownups talk about people they knew, how they wore their hair and the clothes they liked on themselves and their children. I used this mental imagery to make my own designs." In addition to drawing, Kish says, "I always sculpted, even before I knew the word—first in snow, then later in clay. There was never any question, from my earliest memory, that my mode of expression would be figurative."

After completing high school, the artist spent two years at the University of Colorado, followed by two years at the Rocky Mountain School of Art. She began selling her own dolls in 1976, and also sculpted and did costume designs for major collectibles companies, including Effanbee, Enesco Corporation, The Franklin Mint and The Hamilton Collection. Kish introduced her own vinyl dolls in 1990; since then, she has created dolls solely for Kish & Company, established by the artist and her husband, Tamas. Kish does not limit herself to vinyl dolls, however. She works with earth clays, generally stoneware, to create one-of-a-kind pieces—prices for them begin around $3,000—and also issues porcelain dolls. Her porcelains are generally limited to editions of twenty-five to thirty-five pieces and sell for between $350 and $2,500.

Kish's work is not difficult to distinguish, because, explains the artist, "Over the years, I have established an 'identity of design,' that is, whatever I design looks like a family—different but with similarities that identify them as my work. It has been noted that the way I sculpt the lips and paint the eyes are marks of my work. I attach a great deal of importance to the hands of my dolls, as well as to the general proportion. The feet on my dolls are big in comparison to many other dolls, too. This is because, in most cases, I try to come close to natural proportions."

Her subjects range from young to old, male to female, and the emotions her dolls evoke are equally varied. When designing her vinyl line, she says, "I generally do not go in for broad expressions, such as laughter or crying. The faces tend to be wistful, hopeful, melancholy or a bit sad, depending on who is looking at them. I think *Jack* is one of the best examples of this. With my one-of-a-kind pieces, I go for stronger, more specific emotions." An example of this is seen in *Ennui*, a 20-inch stoneware doll that the artist describes as "a portrait of a girl who is bored, even a little amused at being bored."

Kish has been a member of the National Institute of American Doll Artists since 1980. Her dolls are sold in specialty stores around the world, and exhibited in several museums, including the Rosalie Whyel Museum of Doll Art, Bellvue, Washington, and the Musée des Arts Décoratifs, Paris, France.

Jack, 16 inches, vinyl

Ennui, 20 inches, stoneware

Phoenix, 28 inches, stoneware

When Tim Krey gave his wife a doll magazine in 1980, "I couldn't put it down," says Susan Krey. While a lot of the dolls featured in magazines back then were antiques, there was a growing interest in collectible dolls for adults. Companies such as Effanbee, Royal House of Dolls, Seymour Mann and World Doll were issuing collector dolls at that time, and Krey knew that she had the skills to make her own appealing pieces.

Born in London, England, the artist had attended London's College of Art, where she majored in fabric design, and the Royal Society of Arts. After graduation, she went to Australia, where her mother and sister were then living, and began teaching art. Later, she got a job in fabric design, but realized that she enjoyed teaching more, so returned to it. Then American-born Tim Krey entered her life; after their marriage in 1967, they moved to

the United States. Krey spent the next dozen years raising their family of five. Throughout that time, she continued to paint and sculpt, so when she was introduced to collector dolls, she knew she'd found her forte. After all, she had the artistic skills, plus a deep love and understanding of children. What better way to use her talents than making dolls, which, she says, provide "a way to capture those wonderful moments in time that young children bring you."

By 1981, Krey was making and selling her porcelain dolls—selling them so fast that her husband quickly realized that dollmaking was going to be more than a hobby for her. So the Kreys formed the Krey Baby Doll Company, and she has been creating wonderfully realistic porcelain portraits of toddlers and young children ever since. In 1991, Tim Krey quit his job in the aerospace industry to run their thriving doll business. In 1993, Krey did a few designs for The Ashton-Drake Galleries, because she couldn't keep up with the demand for her dolls. But she's happiest when she controls every step of the dollmaking process and can ensure that the dolls meet her exacting standards, so she no longer designs for anyone but her own company.

"I hope my dolls will touch the heart of the collector because of their 'spirit' inside and their decorative value," says Krey, who uses a water-based clay for her original sculptures. She generally creates six or seven new designs a year. These sculptures are then used to make molds for her wax-over-porcelain pieces, which she issues in limited editions of twelve to fifty pieces each. She also does a few one-of-a-kinds. With her training in fabric design and an innate sense of style, Krey makes wonderful use of color and texture in her dolls' costumes. Coupled with her skills at sculpting sensitive, realistic faces, it is not surprising that she has maintained a successful career for two decades.

Olivia is typical of the artist's dolls. The 29-inch, wax-over-porcelain doll has a hard-stuffed cloth body with a wire armature, blown-glass eyes and a human-hair wig. The doll is limited to an edition of thirty-five pieces. Its dress is made of white cotton batiste and features an inset collar of Battenburg lace. Lavender ribbons and bunches of violets adorn her hair and natural-straw poke bonnet. Adding a special touch is her little parasol, which also features Battenburg lace.

Olivia, 29 inches, wax-over-porcelain

I first became interested in creating dolls for my children," says Nancy Latham. "It started with my first born. My son had a little teddy bear, and I made cowboy outfits for it. When my first daughter was born, I began making little dolls and matching outfits for her and the dolls. Then when my other daughter was born, I began experimenting with soft-sculpted cloth dolls. I went on to experiment with different media, but only as a hobby related to making dolls and clothing for my daughters." Friends, however, encouraged her to sell her dolls, so she went to a local craft show in 1989 and sold out. "That gave me the confidence to try other shows," she says. "With ongoing success, I kept moving on to larger shows. I also kept experimenting with different media and methods to create better dolls. The demand for my dolls increased, and before I knew it, a hobby had turned into a business."

Latham may refer to her dollmaking as a business—she sells her dolls under the name Wistful Children—but she still makes the dolls all by herself. She also takes all the photos of her dolls for use in publications. "Few people know that I love photography," says the artist. "I work a lot with black and white, sepia tone and hand coloring. So many passions and so little time," she laments.

While she enjoys taking photos, she also finds pleasure in collecting them. "I have an extensive collection of turn-of-the-century—the nineteenth century—photographs. When I'm designing a new doll, I spend hours reviewing the old photos. The doll may be influenced by the clothing of one child, the hair of another, and the lips and eyes of others. Sometimes, though, I'll be lucky and find the perfect photo," she says. Then, the child in it becomes the model for her next doll.

Latham was born and raised in Cuba. She came to the United States at the age of fifteen on one of the so-called "Pedro Pan flights"—planes filled with children fleeing Castro. When Latham and her younger sister, Maggie, arrived in the United States, they were placed in foster homes. She has had no formal art training, but the fine artistry of her work has brought her recognition in the world of collectible dolls, and her creations have been nominated for, and won, numerous awards. The majority of her dolls depict children between the ages of four and seven. "I think that is the cutest age range. Children that age make the pouty mouth and are very expressive," says Latham.

The artist makes sixty to eighty dolls a year. Some are one-of-a-kind dolls, which sell for between $1,200 and $3,000; the others are limited to editions of three to thirty-five pieces and are priced from $700 to $1,600 each. Most are 21 inches high, and many come with stuffed animals, such as bears or rabbits. "The most challenging part is sculpting," says Latham, who begins each doll by creating an oil-base clay sculpture of its head. She then makes a mold and casts the head in latex; it is covered with cotton knit, which she paints. "In the early years I worked with porcelain, composition and Cernit. But cloth was always my favorite medium," Latham says, who today works exclusively with it.

Monique and *Stitches*, 21 and 16 inches, cloth

Nadine Leëpinlausky

"In my childhood, I liked to play with my dolls and make many different things with my hands. I began learning needlework when I was five years old, and would knit clothes for my dolls, with the help of my mother," says Nadine Leëpinlausky, who was born and raised in Casablanca, Morocco. Later, she had pasteboard dolls for which she designed and cut out paper clothing. Although she had no formal art training, she continued to express herself through various arts and crafts. When she was ten, she won her school's top award for a scene she created out of crumpled paper; it featured a group of children dancing in the country, and was the first of many school projects for which she received prizes. During her teens, she spent her free time decorating her home. She painted murals on walls, did fancy needlework for the draperies and bed covers. Then, at the age of eighteen, she began making cloth dolls, which she sold in shops.

Leëpinlausky moved to France when she was twenty and attended a finishing school for young women in Paris. After she completed her education, she began working  in her family's business. That didn't fulfill her artistic soul, though, so she got a second job decorating shop windows. Marriage and three children slowed her down a bit, but she continued to work in the family business and to paint. Also, she began collecting antique dolls. She loved the dolls, but found many of their faces unattractive. "Then one day I saw some contemporary dolls, and immediately I bought some by different French artists. These dolls were very classical. Later, I discovered Anne Mitrani's dolls, which were extremely realistic. I wanted to buy one of her dolls, but unfortunately they were very expensive. Then, in 1991, I came across information about a doll-making medium called Cernit. Quickly, I went to Paris and bought some. I tried to make a doll, but it was very difficult because I had no information about dollmaking." However, through experimentation, she managed to complete her first doll. She enjoyed the process, and "immediately made many dolls."

After a year of experimentation, Leëpinlausky had her first professional exhibition in Paris. In 1994, she debuted her dolls in the United States, at Deborah Hellman's show in Chicago, where she received considerable attention. In the ensuing years, her adorable portraits of children have brought her international recognition and numerous awards. Her work has been featured in doll magazines here, in Europe and in Japan, and she has exhibited her dolls throughout Europe and in Russia.

Leëpinlausky initially worked in Cernit, but later switched to resin and polymer clay. Today she uses a mixture of three different polymer clays for her dolls, which gives them a transparency similar to a baby's skin. "I work every morning in the family's enterprise. I work afternoons, nights and weekends in my doll studio. I was born in June, so perhaps I have a Gemini's two personalities," she muses, adding, "I work most of the time, but I like this. It is impossible for me to be idle. Even when on holiday at the beach, I knit pullover sweaters or sew dresses for my dolls." By keeping to this hectic, but satisfying, schedule, she is able to make fifty to sixty one-of-a-kind dolls per year, ranging from about 12 to 20 inches in height. Some are completely sculpted; others have heads and limbs made from polymer clay, and stuffed cloth bodies.

Karline, 18 inches, polymer clay

Isinda, 19 inches, polymer clay

*L*isa Lichtenfels has chosen the art of dolls over traditional sculpture because, she says, "traditional sculpture always has one big drawback—tradition. I don't want that baggage. I don't like thinking about all the other artists who have done oil painting or bronze casting before me. I want to do something for the first time. I love invention and innovation! New horizons are what I live for," adds the artist, whose nylon-over-mixed-media dolls are so perfect that, when seen in photos, they are often mistaken for real people.

Perhaps the realism of her pieces is so extraordinary because Lichtenfels admits that "to me, my dolls are real people, and in making them and learning who they are, I understand more of what the world is about. The world is really quite a remarkable, magical place—we just get pulled down by the day-to-day to the point where we don't see it anymore."

To describe a typical Lichtenfels doll is impossible, because she is constantly experimenting, creating new works that evoke the full range of human emotion. She is "not

a fan of style," she says, "because all art comes from nature, and nature does not have a style. Sometimes I think style happens when an artist falls short of nature's perfection. Since we are all human and not as grand as nature, style is inevitable. I work against style and believe that nature is the greatest teacher. I strive to continue to learn and grown, and I hope that dedication is what sets my work apart."

Born and raised in Erie, Pennsylvania, Lichtenfels began making dolls and figures so early in her life that she has "no clear memory of it," but it may have begun with her father's white pipe cleaners that, she says, "I thought I could turn into little skeletons." She attended Pennsylvania Governor's School for the Arts (a high school) and the Philadelphia College of Art, where she earned a B.A. degree and several student honors for her work. Her major was illustration and film making. After graduation, she moved to California and spent a year as an animator apprentice and inbetweener at the Walt Disney Studios in Burbank. During that time, 1980 to 1981, she began selling her dolls. Just a few years later, in 1985, Lichtenfels was elected to the prestigious National Institute of American Doll Artists.

After leaving the Disney Studios, Lichtenfels returned to Erie, then moved to Massachusetts, where she received Massachusetts Cultural Resources Project Grants. From 1986 to 1989, she was Artist in Residence for the Massachusetts Cultural Education Collaborative, and in 2000, she received an Artist Fellowship Grant from the Springfield Cultural Council and the Massachusetts Cultural Council. Other honors include the 1993 Bronze Award for Creative Excellence in Dimensional Illustration at the Fifth Annual Dimensional Illustration Awards Show in New York City, and the Jumeau Award for Leading Female Doll Artist at the 1994 Fourth World Doll Congress in Paris.

The artist's dolls begin with a drawing. Then comes the skeleton, the building up of the muscles and tendons, and finally the nylon "skin." Her understanding of anatomy, coupled with her own exacting standards and her consummate artistry, make her dolls simply astonishing. She has shared her techniques with others through an instructional video made by Rockfish in 1999, and a book, *The Basic Body, Soft Sculpture Techniques of Lisa Lichtenfels*, published in 1995 by Carruth Press. A second book, entitled *Figures Of Fabric: The Sculpture of Lisa Lichtenfels*, was published by Portfolio Press in 2001.

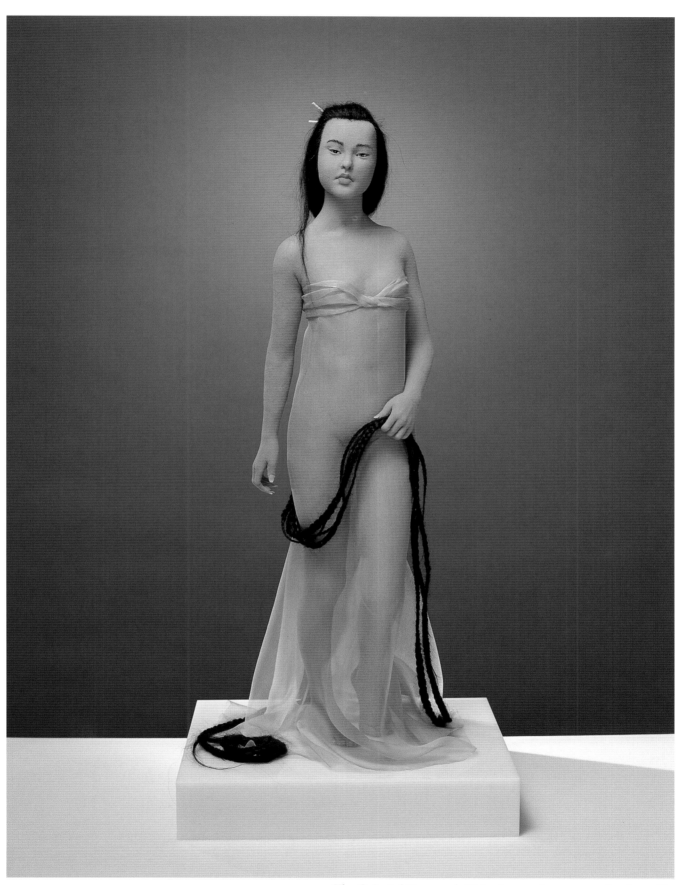

The Oriental Rapunzel, 25 inches, nylon-over-mixed-media

103

Slave Children, 18 and 11½ inches, nylon-over-mixed-media

Angel of Death, 23½ inches, nylon-over-mixed-media

I remember begging my mother for a pillow case to make my 'baby' a dress when I was about four or five years old. When I was nine, I found a washcloth and an old dress and cut out a Santa Claus, sewed it roughly together and stuffed it with bandage cotton. I can't believe that years later making dolls would, once again, become my passion," says Anne Robin Luckett.

A graduate of Mississippi College, located in her hometown of Jackson, Luckett was a fine arts major; she went on to earn two M.A. degrees, one in guidance and the other in art. After teaching art in secondary schools for eleven years, she gave up her career to raise her four daughters. To avoid having to juggle her love for her children with her passion for art—and giving neither the necessary time—Luckett vowed to do no artwork until

she'd raised her children, and she stuck to that vow. Finally, when her girls were young adults, Luckett began making life-size figures to "entertain them and decorate our home." These included a Santa, a butler, an upstairs maid and an Easter Bunny, all decorated with liberal cuttings of hair from her horse's tail. By the time her horse "was bald," she says, "I was excited and ready to move on."

Like many, she discovered the world of art dolls through collector magazines. Luckett began sculpting with polymer clay in 1994, but switched to Cernit at the suggestion of other doll artists. Cernit remains her sculpting medium of choice today. She was accepted into the Professional Dollmakers Guild and exhibited with the group at the 1995 American International Toy Fair in New York City. With her first sale at that show, she says, "I was hooked." In 1996, she made her first limited-edition piece; titled *Anne Clark*, it was nominated for a *Dolls* Award of Excellence. Other honors followed, such as being invited to participate in a fund-raising exhibit for AIDS, held at the Stricoff Gallery in New York City.

As the demand for her work grew, she opened her own studio; today she has several part-time employees, along with a full-time business manager. Luckett creates whimsical dolls, specializing in "lifelike animals and troll-like creatures. I have always been an animal lover," she says, noting that her inspiration for many of her dolls comes from animals. "My studio is a renovated barn out behind my home. I am surrounded by various small animals that inspire me daily," she says.

Luckett creates one-of-a-kind and limited-edition dolls. Her editions are usually limited to twenty pieces. Prices for her work, which is carried in about thirty stores throughout the nation, begin at $800 and go up to over $3,000. *Iris*, a 2001 nominee for a *Dolls* Award of Excellence, is typical of her work. The doll's head, arms and legs are resin; its body is cloth over a wire armature. Issued in an edition of twenty, the self-standing 24-inch doll is dressed in a boucle jumper over a cotton-knit shirt, a cotton petticoat and pantaloons. She wears a jester-style hat and carries a frog jester hand puppet.

Iris, 24 inches, resin

weet and sassy, that's what Jan McLean's dolls are. They're dolls "with attitude"—dolls that capture your attention first, and your heart second. "I adore red hair, rich fabrics, velvets, laces, beads, plumes and blooms," says McLean. "I use a lot of black lace and bright fabrics and hats. I play up the eyes on my dolls, which are fashion dolls, dolls with a touch of the Victorian, a touch of Lolita, plus a dash of passion and romance."

McLean, who was born and raised in Invercargill, New Zealand's southernmost city, is a self-taught artist. Although both her mother and maternal grandmother were artistic—her mother was a painter, her grandmother sculpted—they had pursued careers as nurses, and McLean followed in their footsteps. She was certified as a state registered nurse and spent twenty-two years doing general and obstetrics nursing. During that time,

she married, had four children and began doing pottery as a hobby. In 1983, she decided to make a doll for her daughter. Sculpted from Fimo, "it was gross," she says. She began making reproductions of antique dolls, and opened a ceramics studio with one of her sisters. Then, in 1985, Hildegard Günzel visited New Zealand with Mathias Wanke; when McLean saw her beautiful dolls, she knew she'd never be happy making reproductions again. She had to sculpt her own designs. By 1991, she had created enough dolls to exhibit at the American International Toy Fair in New York City. They were a hit, and she's had difficulty keeping up with orders for her work ever since.

McLean's initial dolls were large, ranging from 28 to 42 inches, and all were made from porcelain. After several years, she added smaller 20- to 28-inch pieces to her line. In 2001, she began reproducing some of her designs in vinyl. She also creates one-of-a-kinds. To meet the demand for her dolls, McLean has hired assistants to help with production. She, of course, does all the original sculpting, using clay and plasticine, although she says that sculpting is her "biggest challenge. I'm slow—but getting faster. Another big challenge is trying to do it all, the designs and the originals." The artist issues two lines of limited-editions: Original dolls, limited to editions of ten to 500 pieces, and Design dolls, issued in editions of 500 to 7,500. While she would like to "do it all," time limitations force her to let her assistants do more of the work on the Design editions. McLean does do all the costuming designing, though, noting that her dolls "are a vehicle for my love of fashion, color and texture."

McLean's dolls have won a number of awards, but even if they had received no recognition, the artist would make them. "Dollmaking is an all-consuming passion, an obsession," she says. "I guess all successful artists are obsessive-compulsive-addictive. I am in awe sometimes myself when a certain doll is an instant 'hit.' What gives a doll that 'X factor' is a combination of face, design and colors. It is a wonderful feeling when a doll is a global success," says McLean, adding: "I love the whole process of dollmaking. Watching an idea evolve—it is almost always a surprise. Breathing life into porcelain is fascinating. I love it when the doll finally 'talks' to me."

Nellie and *Little Nell*, 21 and 16 inches, vinyl

When I was a child in Spain, I liked to make little clay animals from the red clay in the area," says Juanita Montoya, who was born in Barcelona, and lived there until the age of fourteen, when her family moved to Peru. "But what I most enjoyed was sewing, crocheting, knitting, embroidery and fancy needlework. At the Catholic school I went to in Spain, we studied for three hours in the morning. Then, after a break for lunch and a rest, we went back to school and for two hours we did needlework. This was when I was just eight or nine. Then in the summertime, I took white sewing lessons from my father's cousin. Here in the States, you call it French sewing, but we called it white sewing because it was the kind of sewing brides did for their trousseaus. When other kids were outside playing, I went to my white sewing teacher and made things for myself."

After her family moved to Peru, Montoya took secretarial classes, and worked in an office until her marriage, at age twenty-one, to Henry Montoya, a doctor. The couple moved to the United States for two years, then went back to Peru for six before returning to the United States and settling here permanently in 1966. They have three children.

Montoya has always had an appreciation for art, and when her children were young, she decided she wanted to do metal sculpting. "I had no idea how to do it, so I signed up for a soldering class." Still struggling with English, she didn't realize that she'd enrolled in a class for factory workers. "When I told my husband about it, he made me cancel. So I bought myself a soldering gun and decided to teach myself, but I was unable to do it. I needed more hands," she says. Next, she turned her attention to ceramics. "I love the Capodimonte flowers and wanted to make them, so I took a ceramics class. But they didn't use porcelain, saying it was too difficult." Finally, she took courses with Seeley's and Bell Ceramics. "Then I went to the library and got all the books on sculpting and proportion and life studies that I could find, and I practiced and practiced and practiced." Finally, in the early 1980s, she made her first doll, which won an award at the International Doll Association Convention. She's been making dolls—and winning awards—ever since.

Over the years, Montoya has used many media, including Super Sculpey, Fimo, Cernit, porcelain and resin. Then, in 1998, she began working in poured wax, which she currently uses for many of her one-of-a-kind creations. But she also issues some dolls in porcelain editions of twenty-four or twenty-five pieces, and vinyl editions of 100 to 150 pieces. All of her dolls begin as clay sculptures. She then makes a waste mold, casts the doll in porcelain and reworks it. She may repeat this process several times, making new molds from the reworked porcelain piece until she is satisfied with the design. Only then are the molds made for the actual casting of the doll in wax, porcelain or vinyl.

Montoya has created many very appealing dolls of children, but most of her dolls now depict young ladies because, she says, "I have more opportunities to be creative in their costuming." Her 40-inch *Azucena* is typical of her work—large, lovely and beautifully costumed.

Azucena, 40 inches, porcelain

*M*innesota-born-and-bred Sarah Niemela is a relative newcomer to the world of dolls. The artist sold her first one-of-a-kind pieces in the fall of 1997, and she only makes ten to fifteen dolls a year. But the charm and realism of her pieces have brought her national attention—she was the subject of *Contemporary Doll Collector* magazine's January 2001 cover story—and she has a dedicated group of collectors.

Niemela took sculpting classes at art centers in her area and was creating small clay figures when, in the mid 1990s, she bought her first doll magazine and "became totally immersed in doll art. I have always been interested in artworks that depicted the human body, and I knew that I could sculpt," she says, "but I didn't realize how difficult it would be to make a doll!" The artist spent the next year studying children—taking photographs and measuring her own children and her friends' in order to learn about proportion—and working with various sculpting media in her effort to create a realistic portrait.

"Keeping a doll's proportions true to the age of the child I am trying to portray is the most challenging part of dollmaking," the artist says. It's something Niemela has mastered, though; when collectors see her dolls, they almost always comment on how lifelike they are. "I have always been around children," says the mother of thirteen, "so have endless opportunities to observe them. I study the bones and muscles in the faces of children so that I can correctly define them in my dolls. Because I love realism in all forms, I am constantly striving for better form and emotion in my dolls. I want my dolls to communicate with people."

The artist hopes her dolls will speak of the beauty and innocence of childhood. "Children have a whole range of emotions, and I hope to be able to portray all of them, making each doll unique, different from any I've done before. Most people find a familiar face in my dolls," says Niemela, who takes great joy in her craft. "Although I love bronze, the creation of dolls allows me to bring a child to life. Polymer clay so closely mimics real flesh," she notes. "Also, I enjoy playing with color and texture in the hair and clothing." Collectors often forget that dollmakers have to know how to make patterns and sew, as well as style hair. Fortunately, these were skills that Niemela already possessed, having made clothing for her children and cut and styed their hair many times.

Brittany, a 10-inch seated doll, and *Nate*, 18 inches, are typical of the artist's pieces, which sell for $2,300 to $2,500 and are all one-of-a-kind. "I prefer to sculpt children. I love the smooth skin and sweet, round curves of their faces. Also, their fingers and toes are so fun to sculpt," says the artist. Her dolls' heads, arms and legs are made from a combination of Cernit and Super Sculpey. *Brittany* and *Nate* have mohair wigs and blown-glass eyes—unlike her earliest pieces, which had eyes she made herself out of Cernit. Their bodies are Paperclay over plastic foam and wire. *Brittany* is dressed in silk; *Nate* wears a cotton shirt and shorts, a silk tie, cotton socks and clay shoes with leather ties.

Brittany, 10 inches, Cernit and Super Sculpey; Inset: *Nate*, 18 inches, Cernit and Super Sculpey

*M*el Odom created Gene, his first doll, during a difficult time in his own life. "One of my best fiends was very ill, and I spent a lot of time with him in the hospital." Frustrated and depressed after the visits, knowing his friend would not recover, Odom would go to Michael Evert's studio (Evert sculpted Gene for Odom) and work on Gene. The work would snap him out of his depression. "It was the creativity of it all, and working with Michael was so much fun. At that point, I didn't know if Gene would go any further than Michael's studio, but it gave me a focus and a challenge at a time when that was very important to me."

Born in Richmond, Virginia, and raised in Ahoskie, North Carolina, Odom was a successful illustrator at the time he began work on Gene. He had graduated from Virginia Commonwealth University, where he majored in fashion illustration, and done post-graduate work at the Leeds Metropolitan University in England. After moving to New York City in 1975, he did cover illustrations for books, albums and magazines, including *Time* and *Omni*. Also, he was a regular contributor to *Playboy*, illustrating fiction stories. Dolls, which he had played with as a child, re-entered his life in the late 1970s, when he decided to do some illustrations of Barbie.

"I thought of Barbie as the mid-point between Marilyn Monroe and Mickey Mouse as a cultural icon. I bought one from a girl friend, and did two portraits. One of them got published in *Playboy*, as an illustration for a short story." Later, *Playboy*'s art director gave Odom a box full of Barbie dolls that he'd bought at a flea market. "Suddenly, I had a collection of something. I had never collected dolls before, but I got hooked in that way, and I started getting into the minutia of them, the details, the clothes. It's interesting because never in a million years did I think that as an adult I would collect dolls."

Eventually, collecting dolls wasn't enough. "I wanted to create something for myself, and that's how the idea of Gene first occurred to me." From 1991 until Gene's debut from The Ashton-Drake Galleries in 1995, Odom worked on the doll. One of his inspirations was the Théâtre de la Mode exhibition of figures made at the end of World War II to promote French fashions. The restored exhibition was displayed in 1990 and 1991 at New York City's Metropolitan Museum of Art. "I wanted to do Gene in the same period, because I thought the clothes were so beautiful, and they seemed to have a tremendous emotional resonance about them. You've seen your favorite movie stars in those clothes. You've seen pictures of your family in those clothes. They were a part of your consciousness. You had enjoyed those clothes sitting in your pajamas watching television during your childhood. You already loved them." Working closely with Evert, Odom created not only a great face, but a whole persona for his doll, and once it was produced, he and Gene became instant celebrities.

Odom has now designed other dolls, also sculpted by Evert, but Gene seems to mean the most to him. "I created Gene to escape hard times, and I think a lot of people play with Gene for the same reason," he says, adding, "Gene is about optimism. She's about wanting your life to be wonderful, about hoping your life will turn into something amazing. I hope that's her legacy—providing optimism, because I think we all need it, and it's in short supply sometimes."

Gene — Garden Party, 15½ inches, vinyl

Madra Lord — Black Widow, 15½ inches, vinyl

Gene — Blue Fox, 15½ inches, vinyl

Born in Eastbourne, Sussex, England, during World War II, Carol Piper spent her childhood at a time when "dolls were not easy to come by," so she made her own. "I spent hours fashioning dolls out of cloth, plasticine, wood, anything I could lay my hands on. The results were pretty awful," she admits, but that didn't matter. "To me, an only child, dolls were little people, my companions. I also loved history and costume. I spent a lot of time in the public library fascinated by costume books and how-to-make-it publications."

At the age of sixteen, Piper went to work at a small tailoring and dressmaking establishment. "My boss had been a head cutter and fitter with Norman Hartnell, who designed and made clothes for the royal family. Our small establishment also held the Royal Warrant. Learning sewing skills there was another brick in the wall of my dollmaking, though I didn't think about that at the time. I was married at twenty, and dollmaking was put on hold while my three children were growing up, though I did venture into soft dolls for them."

In the mid 1970s, Piper began experimenting with dollmaking. She tried plasticine, papier-mâché and self-hardening clays. Finally, she found a doll club in London, and through the group met other dollmakers and discovered that she could buy porcelain slip. "From then on," she says, "it was all systems go." After buying a kiln and mastering mold making, Piper made her first porcelain doll—a portrait of England's "Queen Mum." Other portrait dolls of the British royal family followed—she began selling them in 1984—and she soon had a dedicated group of collectors. She is a member of the British Doll Artists Association and has had her work featured in its exhibitions.

Today the artist creates dolls of adults and children, and of many races. "From the historical costume point of view, I like making adult dolls. I also do dolls of our royal family. But I have recently started making one-of-a-kind children dolls in Fimo, which have ended up in a loose form of historical dress. I love sculpting children, from tiny to about six years old." The majority of Piper's dolls are one-of-a-kinds, although she does issue one new limited-edition porcelain doll per year. Prices for her one-of-a-kinds begin at $1,200; dolls issued in editions of ten to twenty-five pieces sell for $1,000 to about $1,300. Most of her dolls are between 17 and 27 inches high.

Many of Piper's newest dolls of children wear period costumes. Her 17-inch *Thomas* and *Elizabeth*, for instance, wear silk clothing typical of the mid to late 1700s "I think of them as children dressed for an eighteenth-century masque," notes the artist. The heads, arms and legs of these one-of-a-kind dolls are Fimo; the bodies are cloth over an armature. When looking at these and other Piper dolls, one cannot help but notice the superb workmanship of the costuming, which is not surprising considering the artist's long interest in fashion history and her early training as a seamstress. Still, it is her sculpting that first draws one's attention, especially with her dolls of children. "I find the proportions of children's faces beautiful. I hope to reproduce some of that," she says.

Thomas and *Elizabeth*, each 17 inches, Fimo

*I*n 2000, Heidi Plusczok received not one, but two of the coveted *Dolls* Awards of Excellence. They were not the first awards her work has garnered, nor will they be the last. But they were a nice way to mark the beginning of a new millennium and the German artist's twentieth anniversary as a dollmake—especially since the award winners are selected by collectors, the readers of *Dolls* magazine.

Born in Hanau, Germany, Plusczok "was not an artistic child, but my mother was creative, and I may have inherited some talent from her," she says. "My mother taught me how to sew, and I made clothes for myself when I was a young lady, and for my daughter until she was about ten years old." As an adult, Plusczok grew interested in pottery, and made some clay vases and other decorative pieces. Then, in 1980, she crafted her first doll of Cernit. Within six months, she was selling her one-of-a-kind Cernit dolls in a store in Frankfurt. Meanwhile, she began experimenting with porcelain. Of course, in the early

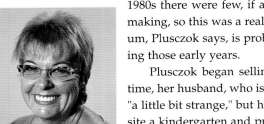

1980s there were few, if any, instruction books or classes in porcelain doll-making, so this was a real challenge. Her determination to master the medium, Plusczok says, is probably what kept her interested in dollmaking during those early years.

Plusczok began selling limited-edition porcelain dolls in 1981. At the time, her husband, who is a teacher, thought dollmaking as a profession was "a little bit strange," but he's very proud of her today. The couple live opposite a kindergarten and public school, so, says Plusczok, "I have lots of children to watch, which inspires me to make dolls of them. I also find inspiration from photographs of children in magazines. Most of my dolls incorporate just an element or two of the child that initially inspired it. For instance, I may be inspired by the character of the child, or by a particular child's smile or eyes. I have made portrait dolls for a few of my collectors, but I prefer to make my own dolls, to bring something of myself into them."

In 1996, Plusczok began designing for Zapf Creations, a German company that issues vinyl dolls. She was impressed with the quality of the vinyl, and was happy to be able to offer a less-expensive doll to her collectors. However, she says, "I always wanted to put my hands on these dolls." Zapf brings Plusczok into its factory to approve the work, but after having had complete control over her dolls for sixteen years, it was difficult for her to leave the finishing work to others. A few years ago, she asked the staff at Zapf if they would do the molding of a separate line of vinyl dolls for her; she would then finish the dolls in her own studio. Zapf agreed, so today Plusczok's dolls are available in two distinct vinyl editions: one from Zapf, which she designs and approves, and one from Heide Plusczok Puppen-Design. She personally finishes each vinyl doll issued under her studio name. "I paint these vinyl dolls, decorate them with wigs and eyes, and I make all of their clothing," says Plusczok. "I believe I am the only artist doing this kind of work on vinyl dolls, and it gives me something special for my collectors." Since these vinyls are selling out in the first six months of each year, it is obvious that collectors appreciate her work. But all her dolls—from the few one-of-a-kinds she makes each year to her vinyl designs from Zapf Creations—are so adorable it would be difficult to not love them.

Natascha, 22 inches, vinyl

Samantha, 23 inches, vinyl

Constanze, 24 inches, vinyl

*R*ita Prescott was born in Wuerzburg, Germany. She studied clothing design and was a certified dressmaker when, in 1983, she married an officer in the United States military. The following year she came to the United States with her husband, Don, who was transferred to Fort Benjamin Harrison in Indiana. The couple lived there for six months, then moved to California. "Don's duty station was Fort Ord, and we lived in Salinas for about three years," says Prescott. "That's where I took some fun classes, to see if I could stand to go back to school. I took basic art, typing, pottery and accounting." Her classes were interrupted when her mother got sick, and she had to return to Germany to care for her. About the same time, she found out she was pregnant with their third son.

After several months in Germany, Prescott returned to California and completed a secretarial course at Salinas College. She also completed her accounting courses through a correspondence school. "Several years later," she says, "I saw a doll collection at a friend's home, and it excited me immediately, although I had seldom played with dolls in my childhood. I started buying molds and making reproduction doll." She enjoyed this, but dreamed of making her own dolls. "I took sculpting classes with Lewis Goldstein in 1992 and 1993. In 1994, I made my first doll, *Ayesha*, and released another, *Ramona*, as a mold." She's continued to make dolls, although she sculpts only two to four new dolls each year, then issues them in porcelain editions of between two and twenty pieces. It's impossible for her to do more, she notes, because she does all the work on the dolls by herself.

"Sculpting with clay gives me the possibility to incorporate all my fantasy and my artistic proficiency," says Prescott. "My dolls portray children, as they are, with all the expressions of joy. I sculpt children of all ages and races. When creating a new doll, I get my ideas from children around me as well as from pictures. The sculpting is the part of dollmaking I love the most. Sculpting portrait dolls gives me the biggest challenge." *Janine*, limited to an edition of ten, is typical of her work. This doll's head and limbs are porcelain; its body is cloth. It has crystal eyes, a human-hair wig, and wears a dress of satin, cotton and antique lace.

The artist's only one one-of-a-kind work is in the Spielzeug-Museum (Museum of German Toy Manufacturers) in Neustadt/Coberg, Germany. It is based on a German quotation, *"Ich mache dich zur Schnecke,"* which means, says Prescott, "I turn you into a snail." The piece depicts an angry man shaking his finger at a child, who is returning into her shell. "The object is sculpted in papier-mâché, the clothing is hardened and painted. The snail with the child's head is also papier-mâché," she says.

Prescott is a member of the Vergand Eurpoaeischer Puppenkuenstler, an association of European doll artists. She has won a number of awards in the United States and Europe for her work, including the Max-Oscar-Arnold (MOA) Award, which she received in May 2000. A politician and merchant, Arnold was "the first to bring out a singing and talking doll. When the city of Neustadt decided to create a doll award, they named it after him because of the good things he did for the city and for his doll business," Prescott says. MOA Awards are given in twelve categories, with just one winner per category, and are among Europe's most prestigious awards.

Janine, 26½ inches, porcelain

*I*n the year 2000, Lynne and Michael Roche celebrated their twentieth anniversary as dollmakers. To mark the milestone, they introduced a collection of dolls based on nursery rhymes. While this was a new subject for them, the sweet, slightly stylized faces of their dolls lent themselves perfectly to portraits of storybook friends. Little Bo-Peep, Jack and Jill, Hansel and Gretl—all were charmingly portrayed. The following year, the English couple took us not into books, but back to the past with several sweet children that appear to have stepped right out of the 1930s. Another popular decade for the doll-making duo is the 1950s. Many of their pieces depict children of that post-war period. "I think the most successful of our dolls have a nostalgic 1950s feel, without being slavish-ly stuck in that era," says Lynne. "This is especially the case with the clothes, which have more fantasy about them than what children actually wore at that time."

The Roches have an affinity for the Fifties, since they themselves were children during that decade. Both were born near London—Lynne in Enfield, Michael in Redhill—

but Michael spent his youth in Kenya. When they finally met in the 1970s, Michael was restoring and selling antique furniture, and Lynne was a student at London's Camberwell School of Art. To help pay for her education, Lynne held various jobs, including selling antique fabrics. Then, she says, "Because I always had a love of dolls and dressing dolls from childhood, I began dealing in antique dolls in the late 1970s. Soon, I wanted to make them, so I began to create reproductions of antique dolls." Michael made molds of some of the antique dolls she had on hand, and they purchased molds of dolls they couldn't afford to buy. Lynne had a grand time painting and dressing her reproductions. But as serious dollmakers often discover, making reproduction dolls can be limiting, so Lynne began making originals. By that time, the couple were married, and with Lynne's very first original doll, they established a unique working relationship.

All Roche dolls begin with Lynne working on the head. Michael then takes over and adds his special touch to the sculpture. Once they've completed it, a mold is made and the head is cast in porcelain, fired and painted. The majority of the bodies and limbs of the Roches' dolls are wood, and have shoulder, elbow, wrist, hip and knee joints. These stur-dy, yet attractive, wooden bodies and limbs allow for maximum flexibility when posing and playing with the dolls. Lynne designs the clothing, exhibiting another special Roche touch; the dolls' costumes are sweet rather than frilly. Often handknit sweaters, vests, scarves and mittens are combined with natural fabrics such as wool and linen. The outfits are adorned with appliqued knitted flowers and figures, or embroidery rather than with ribbons and lace. They are highly detailed, meticulously constructed and include lots of accessories. These are clothes that, if made for real children, would carry designer labels and be coveted by kids and their parents.

As the Roches enter their third decade as doll artists, they continue to find fulfill-ment in their work. They have a dedicated group of collectors here and abroad; their dolls are included in important museum collections, such as the Musée des Arts Décoratifs in Paris; and they enjoy the challenge of combining different art forms into a whole. "One idea always leads to others," says Lynne. "There is so much scope for personal expression."

Ellie and *Louisa*, each 19 inches, porcelain

I began painting and drawing when I was a little girl," says Bev Saxby, who was born in South Australia and raised in Adelaide. As a teenager, she studied music at Adelaide's Presbyterian Ladies College and took courses in dress design and graphic art at the Adelaide Arts College. At the age of seventeen, she moved to Sydney with her parents, and won an art scholarship, "but my social life put studying on a back burner," she admits. Marriage and a "somewhat bohemian lifestyle" in a cottage on the shores of Pittwater that she shared with "native birds, domestic animals and children" followed. Ernst Redl—a well-known and respected artist—lived near her cottage and encouraged her to paint.

Saxby honed her painting skills under Redl's supervision. However, when her children grew up ("I have two daughters, who are busy giving me grandchildren, and they are indeed a delight," she says), she became dissatisfied with her paintings. "I wanted the faces in them to be more 'alive,' so making them in three dimensions became a challenge. I taught myself how to make dolls, and enjoyed doing it," says Saxby, who now teaches dollmaking to other artists. She also continues to develop her own artistry, constantly experimenting with various media.

While best known for her porcelain dolls, Saxby makes appealing felt dolls, and has created some remarkable leather-over-porcelain pieces, such as her 14-inch *Renaissance Painting*. Once she covers a doll's porcelain head with leather, she paints it with oils. Through years of painting with oils on canvas, Saxby gained an expertise that is obvious in her dolls. Especially noteworthy are their hand-painted eyes; to get the look she wants on her porcelain pieces, she may paint and fire a doll a dozen times or more.

People often describe Saxby's dolls as soft and pretty, bearing an ethereal quality. The artist, however, is very down to earth, working long hours on her dolls, teaching, and trying to keep up with her two new "babies," a boxer and a little Aussie terrier. ("As I am only four feet ten inches, when the boxer and I waltz, it is a sight," says Saxby with a laugh.) She continues to do all the work on her dolls by herself, including designing, sculpting, making the molds, pouring and cleaning the porcelain, painting, firing, even sewing each doll's cloth body. Because dollmaking is so labor intensive, she designs just four or five new dolls a year. Generally, one of these is a one-of-a-kind, selling for $1,500 to $2,000; the others are issued in limited editions of five to eight pieces. Prices for them begin around $1,000. Most of her porcelains are 28 to 30 inches high.

Saxby began selling her dolls in 1987; she made her first trip to the United States in the early 1990s. Since then, she has shown her dolls at several IDEX shows and about half a dozen American International Toy Fairs. The artist and her dolls have been featured in major doll publications, and her designs have been nominated for *Dolls* magazine's prestigious Awards of Excellence. While Saxby admits that recognition is nice, her greatest joy comes from "designing a doll and getting that clay to respond to what is in my mind."

Renaissance Painting, 14 inches,
leather-over-porcelain

Lady Elizabeth, 28 inches, porcelain

*T*he only child of a well-known Italian musician, Amedia Scattolini, Laura Scattolini spent her youth accompanying her father on his concert tours throughout Italy and Europe. Rather like Kay Thompson's fictional Eloise, who was raised in New York City's posh Plaza Hotel, luxury hotels were Scattolini's childhood abodes. But unlike Eloise, who befriended, or bedeviled, the hotel staff, Scattolini turned to her dolls for companionship. Just as the hotels in which she spent so much time lacked the coziness of a home, however, so were her dolls richly elegant, rather than comfortable playmates. Dissatisfied with the traditional European dolls of the 1950s, she says, "I began to draw my ideal doll, with the look of a simple child and a lot of dresses for every day." The dolls Scattolini makes today, more than four decades later, are vastly superior to her childhood creations, but they are no less notable for their simplicity and genuineness, which endears them to collectors around the world.

"When a collector thinks about a doll of mine, I hope that he remembers the expression and the emotion of my doll, not just a nice dress," says the artist, who makes just fifteen to twenty dolls a year, each a one-of-a-kind priced between $3,000 and $6,000. She works with a mixture of Cernit and Fimo, and enjoys sculpting a variety of subjects. Creating a doll with expressive eyes gives her great joy, and she also gets pleasure from dressing her creations. An unexpected benefit of dollmaking, she says, is having United States artists, collectors and dealers become "the best friends in the world."

Scattolini was born in Mantua (called Mantova in Italian), an ancient town in northern Italy, surrounded by lakes and rich in Renaissance art and architecture. After completing her high school education, she wanted to study art at a university, but was discouraged by her parents. So she took a job with the government and spent her free time painting. In 1971, she married Sergio Zanini; the couple had two children. While her children were at home, Scattolini continued to work and to paint as a hobby. It wasn't until 1991 that, recalling the dolls of her childhood and her determination to make more realistic playthings, she began to make cloth dolls. They sold well at local crafts fairs, but didn't challenge her artistically, so she began making porcelain reproductions. By 1994, she was tired of re-creating other artists' designs and tried sculpting her own pieces from Cernit. "At the beginning, I found it very difficult to sculpt limbs," she admits, but her determination to master all the disciplines of dollmaking paid off, and later that year she sold her first one-of-a-kind doll. Since then, she has gained international acclaim for her dolls and won several awards, including *Dolls* magazine's 1997 One-of-a-Kind Classic award and the 1999 Collector's Choice award at the Walt Disney World Teddy Bear and Doll Convention.

Soft colors, simple hairdos and oh-so-expressive, but usually pensive, faces—such as seen in *Summer Afternoon*—are trademarks of her work. Both dolls in this piece have dreamy looks, but the redhead just may be thinking up some mischief, while the blond seems a bit more introspective. These 13-inch dolls have cloth bodies over wire armatures, soft eyes and mohair wigs. The 16-inch child in Scattolini's *Comic Book*, on the other hand, is definitely enjoying herself. "It's not usual for me to do a laughing doll," says Scattolini, but the charm of this piece makes one hope she will sculpt many more.

Comic Book, 16 inches, mixed media

PHOTO BY CINZIA GHISI

Summer Afternoon, 13 inches, mixed media

Wildflowers, 23 inches, mixed media

*G*erman artist Rotraut Schrott discovered her artistic abilities in 1980 when she decided to make a little doll for her mother as a Christmas present. "I took an adult education class for handicrafts. There, I realized that I had inherited a talent for sculpting from my father, Ludwig Adam, who was a famous portrait artist," she says. He taught her how to draw and paint, and also taught her the importance of proper proportions. The instructor of the crafts class in which she'd enrolled realized by the end of the second session that there was little she could teach Schrott—so she ended up learning dollmaking through experimentation.

By 1981, Schrott had completed a doll that met her high standards; it featured a young black girl, and was selected for a Christmas exhibition in Munich's Ludwig Beck department store. Since then, her dolls have been included in major exhibits around the world and have won numerous awards. For a period, The Great American Doll Company (GADCO) issued porcelain and vinyl editions of her designs, and some of them, too, won

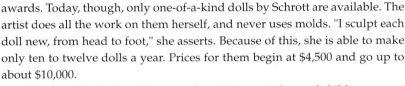

awards. Today, though, only one-of-a-kind dolls by Schrott are available. The artist does all the work on them herself, and never uses molds. "I sculpt each doll new, from head to foot," she asserts. Because of this, she is able to make only ten to twelve dolls a year. Prices for them begin at $4,500 and go up to about $10,000.

"From the beginning, I have preferred to create faces of children, sometimes portraits of real children," says the artist, who shares her hard-learned knowledge of dollmaking in her book titled *Making Original Portrait Dolls in Cernit*. Inspiration for her work comes from observing children—she and her husband Georg have three of their own, now grown—and studying photos of them. What has most influenced her art is her long fascination with the paintings of the Old Masters, such as Rembrandt, Titian and Botticelli. "Velazquez is my favorite," says Schrott, who is particularly taken with "his wonderful paintings of the Spanish king's son and daughter. All my efforts are aimed at sculpting into the faces of my dolls the delicate fineness, the soft-cut features and warm expressions which I admire so very much in the work of the Old Masters."

While Schrott talks about the importance of the facial expressions, collectors of her work enthuse about the great attention she gives to all parts of each sculpture. They extol the very realistic creases and nails on her dolls' tiny fingers and toes; the perfect match of the doll's pose and expression; and the superb complementary nature of the doll's character, the story its face tells, and its costume and accessories.

One can understand collectors' praise when looking at her dolls. For instance, *Bella Anemone* is typical of her work; it is a large doll, 33 inches, depicting a young girl. Its head and limbs are Cernit, which provides a translucency that resembles the glow of healthy young skin, and it has flawlessly painted eyes. Schrott's *Anastasia* is equally appealing, but is an unusual piece for the artist. "This is the first time I've made a young girl, rather than a child, and presented her in a graceful upright position," says Schrott about the 36-inch doll. These dolls are different, and yet they are similar in that every element works together to create what appear to be living, breathing children.

Belle Anemone, 33 inches, Cernit

Anastasia, 36 inches, Cernit

Pamina, 33 inches, Cernit

*R*ustie Siewak grew up with dolls, but they were not companions or playthings; instead, they served as mannequins for her clothing designs. "When I'd get a doll, I'd tear its clothes off, and then I'd search for all the scraps of fabric I could find, and make a new wardrobe for the doll. My mom was really good, because she'd work with me on the sewing," says the artist, whose dolls today wear some of the most sumptuous outfits in the world. Even as a child, Siewak made beautiful clothes for her dolls, although she, herself, was something of a tomboy. When she wasn't drawing, designing and sewing, she was breaking, training and showing Arabian horses.

Born in Aurora, Illinois, Rustie—as she is known to doll collectors—spent her youth in the Prairie State and in Wisconsin. Her artistic talent was recognized by a high school art teacher, who arranged for her to have private lessons. But an early marriage, which ended in divorce, and the birth of her daughter prevented her from furthering her education. She did, however, retain her passion for fashion, and had a successful career designing and making bridal gowns and gowns for competition ballroom dancers.

By the late 1980s, when Rustie made her first doll, she had remarried and was living in Florida. Her husband wanted to semi-retire from his real-estate business, which she'd helped him run, and she was getting tired of designing wedding gowns. "It was hard to put a size 12 into a size 4 gown," she says with a laugh. Also frustrating was when girls insisted on gowns that didn't look good on them. So when Rustie's sister suggested she make soft-sculpture dolls, she gave it a try. At the first doll show she attended, she quickly sold out. Then she met a European dollmaker who asked Rustie to make clothes for her porcelain dolls. She did, but says, "I wanted to do fancy, she wanted plain, so I decided I should make my own porcelain dolls. I found someone to teach me oil painting, and I took sculpting lessons from Hildegard Günzel. I bought books and tapes on doll-making, and got help from everyone I could." Within a year, Rustie was selling her own porcelain dolls, which she lovingly and lavishly costumed.

By late 1995, in addition to making her own limited-edition porcelain dolls, which she sells under the name Rustie's Unique Designs, she was creating dolls for the Home Shopping Network, and appearing with them on television. More recently, and just as successfully, her dolls have been sold on German television. Today, Rustie has three "lines" of dolls: dolls that she designs and makes herself in her Florida studio, which are one-of-a-kinds or editions of five to fifty pieces; dolls she designs and has made overseas for sale through retail stores, which are generally limited to editions of seventy-five to 125 pieces; and dolls she designs exclusively for Home Shopping Network, which are also made overseas. Most are porcelain, but some vinyl editions have been issued.

Rustie's specialty is young women, ranging from 15 to 42 inches high. She finds the most personal pleasure in the large dolls, like the 42-inch bride shown here, because she can really let her creativity flow in costuming them. She adores crystal sparkle organza, sequined and beaded fabrics and laces, and has representatives searching the world over for her fabrics. She also loves jewelry, and personally designs most of the pieces that adorn her lovely ladies.

Bride, 42 inches, porcelain

orn in Salangen, located in the far north of Norway, about twenty-five miles north of the polar circle, Sissel Bjorstad Skille grew up with warm months of light and bitter-cold months of darkness. She enjoyed drawing and modeling, but had no artistic training because no courses were available in Norway's north. "At that time, there were not many dolls to be found in Norway, either," Skille says, but thanks to her enterprising aunts, she had one. "They made Norwegian Selbu knitwear, which they sent to relatives in the United States, and in return they got a real American doll that they gave to me," says Skille. "It was made of composition and had sleep eyes. It was the most beautiful thing I had ever seen. My mother made the most delicate clothes for the doll, exact copies of my own clothes." Today, Skille's mother continues to make dolls' clothing, but now she is assisting Skille with her own dolls.

Although Skille was an education major at Norway's Tromse University, she continued to draw and sculpt. She met her husband in 1970, and after their marriage she began to collect dolls. "I wanted to know more about dolls and ordered a book from England, which contained a chapter about how you could make your own dolls. I started immediately," Skille says. "When I started to make dolls in 1981, the antique dolls were my inspiration, and with my first dolls I tried to imitate the old ones. But as I went on, I got more and more inspired by children's faces and expressions. So my aim changed toward making children as realistic as I could."

During her first few years as a dollmaker, Skille tried many media, including plaster, papier-mâché and, beginning in 1985, porcelain. But when she changed her focus from old-style dolls to realistic portraits of children, she abandoned porcelain for Cernit and Modelene. No longer limited by molds, she found artistic freedom and quickly surpassed her goal of making three-dimensional "photographs" of children caught in special moods.

"Children's faces have always fascinated me. Even when I was a little girl, I had scrapbooks filled with children's faces. Now I use photo albums as my source of inspiration. When I start making a new doll, I usually know what type I want to make, and I start by choosing pictures of different kids that resemble each other, but are shown from different angles." Using these as reference, she then sculpts the doll.

Skille takes "quite a long time" making a doll, so creates only eight to ten a year. She limits her dollmaking to one-of-a-kinds, which are about 30 inches high and sell for $4,000 to $5,000 each. She does, however, create designs for the Götz Company of Germany, which issues vinyls of her dolls in limited edition of 750 each. The subjects of Skille's dolls are usually children between the ages of one and six. "Young children, when they are discovering themselves in connection to their surroundings, fascinate me. I find their innocence and curiosity very touching," she says. *Gina*, *Lisa* and *Sissi* are delightful examples of how Skille captures the fascination of the very young in her work.

Sissi, *Lisa* and *Gina*, 30, 25½, and 29½ inches, Modelene

*W*ith my first tube of red lipstick, borrowed from a friend in junior high school, I became fascinated with the power of female beauty to enchant and transport its observers. I had found a tool of creativity, and the arts seemed my destiny. Thus, I began my long apprenticeship in beauty's tools—fashion, makeup, color and design," says Marilyn Stivers, who holds a B.A. degree from Carnegie-Mellon University in Pittsburgh, Pennsylvania, where she majored in fine arts.

Stivers worked as a professional artist, creating ceramic murals and paintings, until she and her husband—whom she'd married while at Carnegie-Mellon—began their family. The mother of two put her career on hold, because she discovered that she could not be "a good mother and a good artist at the same time. When my younger child went away to school, I began thinking about restarting my art career. With my interest in beauty, fashion and sculpting the female figure, I was only one step away from becoming a dollmaker. However, at the time I didn't even know the world of elite dollmaking even existed," she says.

She was introduced to collectible dolls in the mid 1980s, when a friend took her to a doll show. "I was charmed," she recalls, "and decided to combine figurative sculpting with dollmaking. This was a natural blending of my skills, and this combination has turned out to be ideal for me. It allows me to realize so many of my interests. I continue to use my sculpting ability to explore the myriad possibilities of the female figure and keep on using my vamp's palette of fashion and beauty. When I decided to embark on this path, it seemed a perfectly wonderful, fun thing to do, and it still is."

Stivers, whose dolls are a brilliant combination of innocence and sensuousness, explains that the dolls' sensuality "is achieved primarily from the flow of the body movement and the interplay of positive and negative shapes and spaces." The artist works with synthetic clay and makes one-of-a-kind dolls only, completing approximately fifteen a year. Prices for them begin at $5,000. The most exciting part of sculpting a new doll, she says, is when the face emerges from under her hands. "Up to this point, making her is often vexing and frustrating and mostly technical work. Now I am entranced and enchanted. What will her personality be? Who will she be? Is she a blond? A redhead? I never know, but my hands seem to," she says.

"The greatest challenge for me is to make each new doll a unique personality. I strive to make each doll both an expression of myself and a fully formed individual. I want each of my girls to be a paradox, just as each of us is a paradox. They are refined yet sensual, sensual yet innocent, innocent yet sophisticated, sophisticated yet dreamy, dreamy yet genuine, genuine yet sublime," she adds, noting that she wants her collectors to discover more about the details of her dolls' personalities as they live with them.

Twelve-inch *Leah* is typical of her work. Like all of Stivers' dolls to date, this synthetic-clay girl is one piece; there are no joints, no moving parts, just one fluid sculpture beautifully gowned in vintage fabrics embellished with tiny Swarovski crystal rhinestones, pink opalescent stones and vintage silk ribbon buds.

Leah, 12 inches, synthetic clay

*S*ince 1990, Titus Tomescu has designed a wide variety of dolls for The Ashton-Drake Galleries. He has sculpted dolls of babies and young children, sports figures, biblical personages and blushing brides, like his 22-inch *With This Ring*, which won a 2000 Doll of the Year (DOTY) award. "I don't want to be identified by just one style. I don't want to limit what I do to just one style," says the artist. He does, however, strive for realism in all of his sculptures, while depicting a diverse range of emotions.

Tomescu was born in Timisoara, Romania. His mother, "the intellectual in the family," taught the Romanian language; his father was a wrestling coach and gym teacher, and was one of the Romanians to carry the Olympic torch on its way from Greece to Munich in 1972. Tomescu enjoyed painting and sculpting as a child, and was attending an art-related high school when, in 1982, his parents immigrated to the United States with Tomescu and his younger brother. Because of their democratic leanings, his parents had

lost their teaching jobs the previous year, and it was obvious that life under Nicolae Ceausescu would not improve for them. They settled in Chicago, and after finishing high school, Tomescu attended the University of Illinois. He earned a degree in graphic design, but also took other art and theater courses, including costume design.

Initially, Tomescu worked as a free-lance illustrator, but spent his free time sculpting. "I was working for a publishing company when a co-worker told me that The Norman Rockwell Gallery was looking for a sculptor for figurines. I applied, showed them slides of my work, and the next day I was hired," he says. The Norman Rockwell Gallery was one of the Bradford companies, as is Ashton-Drake. "About a year after I began sculpting figurines based on the illustrations of Norman Rockwell, someone asked me if I could sculpt dolls. Of course I could sculpt dolls," says Tomescu, who spent the next decade creating about a dozen a year for The Ashton-Drake Galleries. Throughout this time, he also did fine-art sculpture, working with various media, including marble, terra cotta and bronze. Like his dolls, the subjects of these sculptures vary, but most are figural; they sell for between $10,000 and $30,000, depending on their complexity.

In spring 2001, Tomescu began developing his own line of dolls, which he personally will issue in limited editions. These new dolls, he says, "will be all age groups and all subject matter. I don't want to stick to just one kind. I'd get bored, and if it's boring to me, it will bore the public." That's something he definitely doesn't want to do, for one of the things he enjoys most about dollmaking is seeing the joy his work brings to others. "Dollmaking can be a pretty lonely job," he says. "You're stuck between four walls seven days a week, and you have to rely on friends dragging you out once in a while to have a good time. You don't really know who enjoys the things you do until you go to a doll signing, and then it's so rewarding. A lot of my collectors were deprived of enjoying a doll when they were little, or they have been traumatized by different experiences as kids or adults. Some of them suffer from the empty nest syndrome—their children have left home and dolls help them recapture memories of their childhoods. It gets pretty emotional, but it's wonderful when my dolls make people happy."

With This Ring, 22 inches, porcelain

I have had a life-long interest in dolls," says Robert Tonner. "I remember being fascinated by the look of dolls and their clothing at a very early age. As I grew up, I had other interests, so it wasn't until I was in my twenties and saw a Sasha doll in a store that my interest was rekindled. I bought one, and started to collect. Before long, collecting wasn't enough. I wanted to express myself through the art of dolls. I tried sculpting my first doll head at twenty-nine—and after that I couldn't stop. I had to make dolls. This was about twenty years ago. Doll art in the early 1980s was beginning to experience a rebirth—there was much great work being done at the time by people like R. John Wright, Helen Kish and Robert McKinley. Seeing this work and getting to know the people who did it really spurred me along."

Tonner, who was born and raised in Bluffton, Indiana, moved to New York City as a young man to study fashion design at Parson's School of Design. After earning a B.F.A. degree, he worked in the fashion industry—first for Gamut, then for Bill Blass. Not long after going to work for Blass, Tonner was made head of the Blassport label. By 1983, he has his own label: Robert Tonner for Tudor Square. Meanwhile, he spent his free time making dolls. Slowly, they, too, began receiving recognition from collectors and other doll artists. By 1985, Tonner's Tudor Square line had lost its backing and he was working for Breckenridge; that year he also began selling his dolls. While his career in fashion had its ups and downs, his progress as a doll-maker was definitely on an upswing. In 1988 he was elected into the National Institute of American Doll Artists, and by 1991 he was able to abandon the fickle world of fashion and found his own doll company—Robert Tonner Doll Design.

"The dolls I create are meant to be played with and touched," says Tonner, who brings great style and sensitivity to his designs, making them appealing to adults and children alike. "I think that there is a connection or bond that develops between a doll and a collector that just can't happen with traditional art. A doll can become a friend—and as I sculpt a doll, I get to know it—it really comes to life." The artist uses Plastilina for his original sculptures, of which he does four to six a year. For these dolls, however, he creates between seventy-five and one-hundred outfits annually. These designs are issued by his company in both open and limited editions—some very small editions of fifty or fewer pieces, others in editions of 3,000 or more.

Since he debuted his dolls at the American International Toy Fair in New York City in 1992, Tonner has created dolls ranging from small children to fashion figures, such as his Tyler Wentworth doll. In discussing his art, he says, "My interest is above all a play-doll style, and what I bring to that classic style is a realism that most play dolls don't have. I like a pleasant, serene expression and contemporary, classic clothing. The line of the dolls is idealized and simplified—and the subject matter usually has something to do with fashion."

Midnight Garden Tyler Wentworth, 16 inches, vinyl

American Beauty Kitty Collier, 18 inches, vinyl

Fleurs du Mal Tyler Wentworth, 16 inches, vinyl

nother of the early German contemporary doll artists, Ruth Treffeisen was born in Lindau. The first of her parents' six children, Treffeisen spent her youth playing with babies, rather than dolls. As her siblings grew, she made toys for them, as such items were hard to find in post-war Germany. At the age of twelve, Treffeisen went to France, where she lived with an aunt in Valenciennes and attended a private girls' school. The school had a good arts program, and her talent was recognized and encouraged by instructors there. Later, back in Germany, a home-economics teacher taught her sewing and fancy needle-work, at which she also excelled.

Treffeisen didn't think of a career in the arts or fashion, however. She trained as a nurse and worked as a geriatric nurse and therapist for fifteen years. As part of her therapy duties, she taught handicrafts to her patients. Married and the mother of three, she also made craft items as gifts for her children.

It was in the mid-1970s when Treffeisen made her first doll as a decorative accessory for her own home. With that first piece—a Cernit fairy—she was "hooked." Then she saw an antique porcelain doll, and was so captivated by its beauty that she knew she wanted to work in porcelain. However, as Hildegard Günzel and Rotraut Schrott also discovered, there were no ready supplies or instructional material for dollmakers in Germany at that time. Determined to create porcelain dolls, she eventually found a ceramics professor who taught her about porcelain slip and mold making. Thus began a period of trial and error, including molds that simply wouldn't open.

Treffeisen began selling her dolls in 1980. "Sculpture and painting were and still are a means for me to express myself artistically; however, I put my soul into my dolls," says the artist. The artistry and high quality of her work, from the sculpting through the costuming, have earned her many awards, beginning in 1986, when her dolls were honored with both first and second prizes from the Doll Artisan Guild international competition.

Because of the demand for her dolls, in 1992 Treffeisen created some designs for The Franklin Mint and for Victoria Impex. Also in 1992, she began issuing vinyl editions of her designs, because she believes that all dolls should be played with, whether they are in the hands of adults or children. Treffeisen sculpts in Plasticene and clay, creating about ten new designs each year. Once a sculpture is completed, she decides if it will be produced as a porcelain or vinyl doll; she never produces a design in both media. Her porcelain pieces are generally limited to editions of ten to 120 pieces; her vinyl editions are larger, ranging from one hundred to 1,000 pieces. On occasion, Treffeisen makes a one-of-a-kind, but it is usually for a special exhibit or fund-raising charity event. Her dolls depict many age groups, except for newborn babies; she is best known, however, for her tender depictions of children, such as *Hannah*. This 30-inch doll, issued in an edition of thirty pieces, has a hand-knotted human-hair wig and blown-crystal eyes. About her accessories, the artist says, "*Hannah* does not go to bed without her bear Amanda, her doll Dora and her little good-night story."

Hannah, 30 inches, porcelain

$\mathscr{M}$y father was a band director and an art teacher. I was a student of his for twelve years, at school and at home," says Indiana-born-and-bred Virginia Ehrlich Turner. Since she was surrounded by music and art throughout her formative years, it's not surprising that she would have a career in the arts. However, while Virginia loved to paint and also enjoyed making clothing for her daughters and their Barbie dolls, it was only by chance that she began designing and sculpting dolls.

In 1980, Virginia's sister-in-law, dollmaker Judith Turner, ran into production problems and asked Virginia and her husband, Boyce, for help. They set up a basement workshop and began producing bodies for Judith's dolls; soon, they were producing all of Judith's porcelain dolls. "I found that I loved creating dolls," says Virginia, who began making dolls on her own as well as helping Judith. "At first, I made only reproductions, because I didn't sculpt. We started Turner Dolls to make Originals by Judy and reproductions by me; mine were called Virginia's Very Own. We started selling our dolls in 1981."

It wasn't long before Virginia began sculpting her own dolls, though, and before the 1980s ended, she was winning awards for her creations. By the early 1990s, Judith withdrew from the business, and Virginia became the company's sole sculptor. She and Boyce added vinyl dolls to their line, and also added staff to meet the growing demand for Virginia's baby and toddler dolls—the age she's most comfortable sculpting. "For much of my life, I have been surrounded by children," explains the artist. "First, I had five younger siblings, then I had three daughters, and now I have nine grandchildren." She believes that art provides a way of seeing the beauty of the ordinary in life. Thus, when she designs a doll, she strives for a very realistic look. She makes large dolls—dolls that are, or come close to, the size of real babies and toddlers—and when designing costumes for them, she selects styles and fabrics that real children would enjoy wearing.

Virginia uses water-based or plastic-based clay for her original sculptures, the vast majority of which are then reproduced in limited editions. The vinyl pieces produced by Turner Dolls are generally limited to editions of 200 to 300. Some of the baby dolls, however, are issued in open editions. Virginia also sculpts dolls for The Ashton-Drake Galleries, and designs a special line of dolls for the QVC television shopping network. All this keeps her busy, but after more than twenty years of dollmaking, she's still having fun. "The most exciting part for me is having my sculpt reproduced in porcelain. That is when it begins to look realistic, and when I can see how I want to dress the doll," she says, adding, "Creating a new doll is very thrilling."

The joy that she finds in her artistry comes through in her dolls, many of which are laughing or smiling. Occasionally, though, she gives some dolls a more pensive or sober expression, which she says, "makes you feel protective of them." Whatever the emotion her dolls evoke, as an artist, her goal—and the reason she periodically takes sculpting classes to keep herself challenged and keep her artistry fresh—is to give collectors dolls that will be "something pretty to look at for a long, long time."

Mona and Celadon, 32 and 33 inches, vinyl

*I*n 1974, Bets van Boxel painted a portrait of a man she wanted to capture in three dimensions. "He was a homeless man," she says, "and I wanted to portray every detail of his clothing and his belongings." She sculpted his head, hands and feet, using a self-hardening clay, and then fashioned a body and dressed the piece. That was her first doll, and she's been making and selling dolls ever since. "With dollmaking, I can make the person really detailed and lifelike," says van Boxel, adding, "I like the different techniques involved with dollmaking, too, such as sculpting, painting, making the clothing and making accessories."

Van Boxel was born in Waspik, Holland, during World War II. She enjoyed painting and drawing in her childhood, and hoped to study art, but her mother felt she should master something that would be of use when she married, so she learned needlework. At

the age of fourteen, she became a professional seamstress. Once she married Jos van Boxel, though, she began painting again. Her husband was also artistic, and the two took evening classes at a local cultural center. She studied drawing and portrait painting; he took classes in pottery making, sculpting and woodcarving. Throughout this time, van Boxel also worked as a seamstress, making coats, wedding dresses and costumes for her clients.

Once van Boxel began making dolls, her husband learned how to make molds, so she could reproduce her original sculptures in porcelain. He continues to assist her with her dollmaking, as does Amy van Boxel, one of their two daughters. Since 1986, when the couple opened De Poppenstee—a gallery featuring van Boxel's work, a shop offering dollmaking supplies, and her studio—the artist has concentrated on sculpting portraits of children, or mothers and children. She and her husband travel extensively, and the children of other cultures that she sees on their trips abroad inspire her work. "I call my dolls 'children of the world,'" she says. "Most of the time, I portray the children in traditional clothing. Whenever possible, the fabrics I use are authentic, purchased in the country during our travels there." Van Boxel also looks for accessories in these foreign countries, and for books that portray the people and can be used for reference. In addition, she takes lots of photographs of the children she and her husband encounter when abroad.

The artist sculpts with Plasticine, then reproduces her dolls in porcelain, limiting her editions to five or ten pieces. Prices for them begin at $1,950. She completes ten to fifteen sculptures a year. "After twenty-seven years, I still make dolls because it is my hobby," she says. "It is nice that I am able to make a living out of it, but I could not create if that were my primary reason for it. What I enjoy is the thrill of starting with some clay and fabric and ending with a complete doll that I made all by myself." Her biggest challenge, she says, is "to improve myself even after all these years."

When one looks at van Boxel's sensitive portraits of South American, Asian and African children, such as *Yoli*, a portrait of an Ethiopian child, it is difficult to imagine improvement is possible. This beautifully sculpted, 17-inch squatting doll is typical of her work. *Yoli*'s head, arms and legs are porcelain; its body is part porcelain and part cloth. Like all Bets van Boxel creations, it has crystal eyes and a human-hair wig.

Yoli, 17 inches, porcelain

Sun Lan, 20 inches, porcelain

A native of Rochester, New York, Jamie Lynn Williamson studied to be a dental assistant and began her professional career working for a children's dentist. It took just a year, though, for her to realize "this wasn't the career for me. I went on to floral design school, and later opened my own flower and gift shop. My first dolls were cloth dolls made for my shop," says the artist, who had enjoyed painting, sewing and drawing as a child. She gave up her shop after the birth of the first of her four children, but continued to make cloth dolls and sell them to stores in the area.

Early in 1997, Williamson was looking through a doll magazine in the hopes of getting some ideas for ways to improve her cloth dolls, when she "discovered what the world of one-of-a-kind doll art was all about. I was so fascinated with what was being cre-

ated, that I decided to give sculpting a try." She loved working with various sculpting media, and abandoned her cloth dollmaking for creating one-of-a-kind Cernit pieces. Today she creates twelve to fifteen dolls a year; prices for them begin at $2,800. Making even that many is something of a juggling act, as her dollmaking takes second place to her family. Fortunately, her husband is very supportive of her artistry and understands when she gets up in the middle of the night to work on dolls.

Williamson learned to sculpt through trial and error, and talking with other artists. "When I began sculpting, someone remarked that my dolls' hands were misshapen. At first, I was devastated by the comment," she says, but after taking a critical look at her work, she "vowed to sculpt more realistic hands. I spent several months working on nothing but that." The result: "Today, when people see my dolls they always comment on the smooth finish and realistic-looking hands," she says, adding, "I am grateful to God for giving me the talent to create these works of art."

For Williamson, the joy of dollmaking is "to begin with nothing but a lifeless lump of clay and slowly see it evolve into the face of a young girl who almost seems alive. I rarely work from photographs, finding it much more fulfilling to begin without any pre-conceived notions of what the doll will look like. I enjoy sculpting all the various ethnic groups." The artist's early pieces depicted children between the ages of two and six, but since 2001 most of her dolls have represented thirteen- to seventeen-year-old girls. Her 24-inch *Alessandra* is typical of this age group. It has a Cernit head, with German glass eyes, Cernit arms and legs, and a cloth body. Also typical of the artist's work is *Alessandra*'s elaborate gown, made of raw silk and antique lace.

"I almost always use raw silk for my dolls' costumes," says Williamson. "I love the warm, soft look it gives my dolls. To complement this rich fabric, I use antique lace for the trim. I spend a lot of time searching the antique stores and flea markets in the area for materials." Her dolls' wigs are made of mohair, human hair or a combination of the two. To enable collectors to pose her dolls, she uses a wire armature inside their cloth bodies.

Alessandra, 24 inches, Cernit

Zofia & Henry Zawieruszynski

orn and raised in Poland, Zofia and Henry Zawieruszynski met when they were in their early twenties. Zofia had attended a five-year art school in Naleczow and worked briefly designing for a children's theater in Warsaw, before returning to her hometown of Stalowa Wola. Henry had studied art in Jaroslaw, and was working in a small shop in Stalowa Wola, designing and painting cotton and silk fabrics. They met in the shop, married in 1971, and quit their jobs to open their own interior-design studio. In addition to designing homes and offices, they created sculpture and paintings; Zofia also designed children's clothing. The couple had two children, and life was good.

Then, in the 1980s, political unrest in Poland caused their business to falter. Supplies were limited, and art took a necessary back seat as people struggled to survive. At the urging of relatives in the United States, the Zawieruszynskis came here in 1988 to look for work, assuming they would eventually return to Poland. They settled in Minnesota, near Henry's relatives, and got jobs with a printing company. They spent their free time painting, and made enough from the sale of their art to quit their jobs and even buy a house, so they once again had studio space.

"In 1992, we were asked to create prototypes of porcelain dolls for a ceramic studio. It was the first time in our lives that we saw collector's dolls," says Zofia. "We designed five dolls for this company, but the arrangement with them did not work out. So we took our first dolls to a local show in Minnesota, and we won the top award there!" Encouraged, the couple made more dolls, went to more shows, and won more awards. Within a decade of seeing their first art dolls, the Zawieruszynskis had their work honored with awards and award nominations twenty-nine times.

"We did a lot of other things in the art world, but after making our first dolls, we never wanted to stop," says Zofia. "It is the passion that fuels our lives. We think that designing dolls is truly our destiny." With their education and background in painting, sculpture and design, they bring a great combination of skills to dollmaking. Their dolls are remarkable for their realism, their poignant expressions and the way every detail enhances the overall piece.

"We try to create dolls that appear to have heart and soul. We try to capture a moment of happiness, sadness, to capture a moment in time," Zofia says. Because of the time they spend on each piece, the Zawieruszynskis create just eight to ten new dolls a year. They issue these dolls in porcelain editions of five to thirty-five pieces. Generally, Zofia does the sculpting of each doll, Henry makes their molds, and together they clean the greenware—the unfired porcelain clay—and complete the dolls. Zofia designs the dolls' costumes, but they select fabrics together. Zofia then creates the patterns for the clothing, while Henry makes the accessories. He also handles the sales and marketing of their creations.

Thirty-two-inch *Matylda* is typical of their dolls, which range in height from about 25 to 32 inches. The doll's head, arms and legs are porcelain; it has a cloth body with an armature. Limited to an edition of twenty-five, *Matylda* wears a white dress trimmed with embroidered lace, a black velvet vest and black porcelain boots. Her accessories include two tassel dolls.

Matylda, 32 inches, porcelain

Directory of Artists

Ardis
123 Shalako
Kerrville, TX 78028

John & Angela Barker
62 Woodside View
Cottingley, Bingley
West Yorkshire BD16 1RL
England

Maja Bill-Buchwalder
Hauptstrasse 27
CH-2553 Safnern/Biel
Switzerland

Pauline Bjonness-Jacobsen
Pauline Collectibles
1 Corporate Dr.
Grantsville, MD 21536

Stephanie Blythe
PO. Box 1806
San Anselmo, CA 94979

Marilyn Bolden
2286 Alligator Creek Rd.
Clearwater, FL 33765

Antonette Cely
3592 Cherokee Rd.
Atlanta, GA 30340

Anna Chapman
3600 Peoria Rd.
Orange Park, FL 32065

Steve and Angela Clark
Still Life
6 Park Rd.
Bowral, NSW 2576
Australia

Berdine Creedy
5015 N.W. 71st Pl.
Gainesville, FL 32653

Paul Crees and Peter Coe
85 Severn Rd.
Weston Super Mare
North Somerset BS23 1DS
England

Edna Dali
17a Hatayasim St.
Ra'anana 43264
Israel

Eileen De Vito
Dolls by Eileen
23 Strawberry Ln.
Huntington, NY 11743

Peggy Dey
2909 Oxford Rd.
Lawrence, KS 66049

Val Ellick
2 Libra St.
North Balwyn, 3104
Victoria
Australia

Yvonne Flipse
Roelshoekweg 14
4413 NG Krabbendinke
The Netherlands

Tom Francirek and Andre
Oliveira
96 Albert St.
Fort Erie, ON L2A 5L1
Canada

Elissa Glassgold
3 Surrey Rd.
Elkins Park, PA 19027

Julie Good-Krüger
136 Stoneyhill Rd.
Qarryville, PA 17566

Hildegard Günzel
Dr.-Alfred-Herrhausen-Allee 60
D - 47228 Duisburg
Germany

Ella Hass
Aalevej 9
7180 Toerring
Denmark

Héloïse
18 Rue Guiillard
44100 Nantes
France

Margie Herrera
RR1, Box 530-C
Kula, HI 96790

Annette Himstedt
Annette Himstedt
Puppenmanufaktur
Karl-Schurz-Str. 27
D-33100 Paderborn
Germany

Maggie Iacono
2 Raymond Circle
Downington, PA 19335

Hanna Kahl-Hyland
200 West Woods Rd.
Hamden, CT 06518

Diane Keeler
1972 300th Ave.
Luck, WI 54853

Helen Cunalta Kish
8250 West Coal Mine Ave., #10
Littleton, CO 80123

Susan Krey
15212 NE 195 St.
Woodinville, WA 98072

Nancy Latham
409 Belle View Ave.
Temple Terrace, FL 33617

Nadine Leëpinlausky
13 Route De Poitiers
86800 Saint Julien L'Ars
France

Lisa Lichtenfels
PO Box 90537
Springfield, MA 01139

Anne Robin Luckett
502 Brame Rd.
Ridgeland, MS 39157

Jan McLean
255 Hillside Rd.
South Dunedin 9001
New Zealand

Juanita Montoya
1437 Blue Jay Circle
Weston, FL 33327

Sarah Niemela
10500 Trail Haven Rd.
Rogers, MN 55374

Mel Odom
GENE by The Ashton-Drake
Galleries
Gallery Marketing Group
9333 N. Milwaukee Ave.
Niles, IL 60714

Carole Piper
73 Fairlawn Dr.
East Grinstead
Sussex RH19 1NS
England

Heidi Plusczok
Erlenweg 5
D-61130 Nidderau
Germany

Rita Prescott
Birkenhainer Str. 530
63450 Hanau
Germany

Lynne & Michael Roche
2 Lansdown Terrace
Lansdown Rd.
Bath BA1 5EF
England

Bev Saxby
10 Namatjira St.
Paradise Point
Queensland 4216
Australia

Laura Scattolini
Via Conciliazione 61
46100 Mantova
Italy

Rotraut Schrott
Spitzingstrasse 1
85598 Baldham
Germany

Rustie Siewak
Rustie's Unique Designs
1573 Coachmakers Lane
Clearwater, FL 33765

Sissel Bjorstad Skille
Nidaroygt. 4
7030 Trondheim
Norway

Marilyn Stivers
PO Box 81309
Wellesley Hills, MA 02481

Titus Tomescu
PO Box 934
Wood Dale, IL 60191

Robert Tonner
459 Hurley Ave.
Hurley, NY 12443

Ruth Treffeisen
Amselweg 13
87487 Wiggensbach
Germany

Virginia Ehrlich Turner
PO Box 36
Hentonville, IN 47436

Bets van Boxel
't Vaartje 14
5165 NB Waspik
The Netherlands

Jamie Lynn Williamson
3505 Lake Rd.
Williamson, NY 14589

Zofia & Henry Zawieruszynski
3901 Main St. N.E.
Blaine, MN 55449